MW00423107

A Path to Joy

A Path to Joy

*God's Way to Live
with More Happiness
and Fulfillment*

DAVID BERNARD

RESOURCE *Publications* · Eugene, Oregon

A PATH TO JOY
God's Way to Live with More Happiness and Fulfillment

Resource Publications
An Imprint of Wipf and Stock Publishers
199 W. 8th Ave., Suite 3
Eugene, OR 97401

www.wipfandstock.com

PAPERBACK ISBN: 978-1-6667-8406-0
HARDCOVER ISBN: 978-1-6667-8407-7
EBOOK ISBN: 978-1-6667-8408-4

VERSION NUMBER 103023

To my loving wife, Jess. You stood with me in the tempest until the winds retreated. And to my children, Ian and Julia. You accepted and believed in me throughout life's many changing seasons.

Contents

Preface

WE ALL GO THROUGH trials, but that doesn't mean we have to lose our joy. I wanted to write this book to encourage those who have been going through difficulties but have lost hope. It's easy to get discouraged when we face trials. Sometimes, we think all we need is a good break and we'll be happy. But often, good breaks don't seem to come.

So, how are we supposed to have joy when we go through hardships?

That's why I wrote this book.

This book shows a way that we can keep our joy no matter what we face. It tells us that no matter the challenge, we can have joy and that hardships don't have to stop before we find happiness.

We all go through trials, but that doesn't mean we have to lose our joy. I want to show you how to have joy despite your difficulties. This means you can have happiness and fulfillment right now. My ultimate hope is for you to find happiness when you read this book and for this joy to last you through your trials.

I face trials like every believer, and I too have questioned if we can have joy in difficult times. But through my challenges God has taught me that he is enough! And that he is all I need to be content, no matter what difficulty I face. He has also taught me to trust him, even when he leads me into the unknown. I am learning to embrace his will, regardless of discomfort. That's because in the end, his plan brings life and peace.

These are the principles I share in this book.

Introduction

BELIEVERS FACE MANY OF the same troubles that unbelievers face, but there is a difference. We have God dwelling in our hearts. That means God's presence is always with us. And because he is with us, we can have joy no matter what we experience.

The truth is we weren't meant to be sad, depressed, or defeated. In fact, God wants us to have joy. And there is no greater joy than to truly know him. Even though adversity makes us uncomfortable, our trials teach us about his faithfulness.

In this book we learn how to have joy and happiness no matter what we go through. This joy comes from knowing that God will not leave us to face our challenges alone. That he will be with us to give us strength. We also discover that everything we need has already been provided by God. And when we follow his plan, we find happiness.

There are many books written about joy and happiness. That means happiness is something people are searching for. So, it seems we all want to have joy, especially in tough times.

Certainly, this book will help! And it will live up to that promise. This book draws us into a more dependent relationship with God. In other words, we do not have to do anything to find happiness. Instead, there is something we must lose. We must lose ourselves in God's will. Which means we must become completely dependent on God, trusting in his provision alone.

When faced with hardships, we often think that our problems are too difficult and will never change. But there is good news! They can change and we can overcome.

We need to start saying, "I am an overcomer!"

Yes, we can get to the place where our weaknesses no longer interfere with our happiness. Even though we may have struggled in the past, now we can confront our weaknesses and find fulfillment. And we confront our weaknesses by embracing the truth. So, as we embrace God's truths, things begin to change.

What Is Fulfillment?

Fulfillment is a result of being changed to reflect God's nature. We do this by following Christ's example. Jesus gave us an example of how to trust in God. And when we place our trust in God, we are assured that he will be faithful to give us strength for every circumstance. That means God becomes the source of our strength and the ultimate source of our happiness.

We find happiness when our sole desire is to fulfill God's plan. But we don't act alone in this pursuit. For God compels us to surrender our hearts. Now, our role is to respond to his call and become totally dependent on the Spirit.

When we are totally dependent on the Spirit, we are sustained only by those things God provides. We must realize that God wants us to depend on him for all our needs. This is so we can learn of his goodness and faithfulness.

Also, being assured of God's goodness helps us have confidence that nothing will bring us eternal harm. In fact, his methods have eternal purpose. That means we find happiness, peace, and contentment at the center of his will.

It is tempting to avoid God's will for the sake of comfort. This, however, does not bring about true happiness. Many times, we create more problems when trying to escape his will. But if we embrace his ways, he will reward us with his presence. And being in his presence is all that is needed to have joy and gladness.

We may not reflect Christ in every area of our lives at this moment, but that's okay. We are a work in progress. Remember, God is patient and understanding. He also knows our limitations.

Even when our circumstances appear overwhelming, we have hope. Our hope is in God who promises to provide a way for us to endure. We know he can do the impossible and will preserve us by his power. And we will never regret placing our trust in him because he is faithful and will never fail.

Chapter 1

Experiencing Joy Every Day

ALL CREATION IS UPHELD by God's power. Not only is he holding worlds together, but he's faithfully watching over every one of us. He pays close attention to each of us and plans to bring good things into our lives. God wants us to enjoy what he has made, but instead of being filled with joy, our lives are often filled with frustration. This daily struggle can be overwhelming and can cause us to forget about the beauty of our existence.

Truly, there is beauty in our existence since we can experience joy in everyday circumstances. Even in the stressful ones. Despite our troubles we can achieve happiness, contentment, and satisfaction in life. That's because God promised that we can have joy right in the middle of our hectic lives. But finding contentment when times are tough can only be accomplished as we draw close to him.

We might ask, "Is it really possible to have joy in every situation?" Yes, it's possible, but we might need a better understanding of what joy looks like.

Joy isn't about getting everything we want or about living free from discomfort. Joy is about being near God while we're going through difficulties. In other words, if we're content to always be with God then we'll always have joy. And we'll always have joy because he never leaves our side.

It's easy to believe happiness is meant for other people and that we'll never be happy or fulfilled. But the good news is God's blessings are intended for us, right now. Although it may take some time to change these negative thoughts, we can start today by applying God's truths to our situation.

Learning to embrace truth helps us become happier and more satisfied in life. Sure, we've heard these claims before, but embracing God's truths helps us live with more peace and joy. However, this happiness comes only from God using our difficulties to develop character in our lives.

Difficulties are often God's chosen method to bring about change. That's because with every hardship comes an opportunity to trust him. And when we overcome our adversity in faith, he blesses us with peace and happiness.

False Beliefs and the Way We See Life

Thinking that we'll never be happy or that life's just too tough interferes with our joy. Even though we confess words of faith, this doesn't stop doubt and fear from attacking our minds. But when we embrace truth, the Spirit replaces these old ways of thinking with a mindset that's focused on God. And as doubtful thoughts are removed, our mind refocuses, and joy starts to emerge again.

It's true. What we believe determines whether we have joy. If we center our beliefs on the truth, we will have happiness. But if our beliefs are influenced by doubtful thoughts, we will experience negative emotions. And if doubt dominates our thoughts, we can start to believe things that aren't true about God, life, and ourselves.

So, if we start to doubt our self-worth, we may believe things like "I'm unlovable" or "I don't matter." And if these beliefs about ourselves are not confronted with the truth, we'll be convinced these beliefs are, in fact, true. Even though we may not say openly that we feel unloved or that we have little value, we can secretly believe they're true in our hearts and lose our joy.

These wrong beliefs can affect our relationship with God and the way we see life. In other words, believing we are unlovable can lead us to assume that God doesn't love us. And if he doesn't love us, can he really be trusted?

We can see how believing "I'm unlovable" impacts our relationship with God. For it questions his love for us and compromises our devotion to him. But when we're fully convinced of God's unconditional love, wrong beliefs are exposed and uncertainty is removed.

Balancing Our Emotions with the Truth

God's truths should be viewed from an eternal perspective. We see this in Isa 55:8, "For my thoughts are not your thoughts, neither are your ways my ways, declares the LORD."

When we place our knowledge above God's truths, it leads to wrong beliefs. Then these wrong beliefs cause us to question God's motives. Which weakens our devotion to him. And since we are easily led away from the truth, God uses our circumstances to help us understand his ways. So, the more we understand, the happier we'll be.

However, we can only be happy if we are willing to let him change us as we go through the tough times. But this change must take place within our hearts if we are to have joy and gladness. In Mark 7:21 we read, "For it is from within, out of a person's heart, that evil thoughts come." By this we see the heart represents the place of our deepest desires. And thoughts reflect what is in our hearts. So, our deepest desire must be to experience real transformation from the inside out. It is this sincerity that leads to true satisfaction in life.

Confronting Negative Thoughts with the Truth

Sometimes, thoughts can be difficult to control. But thoughts of doubt and defeat can be overcome by focusing on God's truths. To gain control of our thoughts we must find out what the truth says about our situation.

We might think there is no way to make it through our problems, but God tells us that "we are overcomers," "we will not be defeated," and "we can have abundant joy!" Once we know the truth, we must choose to believe it.

Strangely, our beliefs do not automatically align with what God says is true. But to overcome our negative thoughts, we first need to know what God says. And if our thoughts are different, then these negative thoughts and wrong beliefs must be surrendered.

Sometimes, our emotions don't agree with what God says is true either. But just because we feel a certain way doesn't make it right. Sometimes, we can feel one way, but God's truths tell us something different altogether.

In other words, we may not feel very strong right now, but the truth tells us we are overcomers! We may not feel like it's possible to get through our challenges, but the truth says that we can endure any hardship! Or we may not feel one ounce of joy, but the truth promises happiness and contentment!

No matter how logical our arguments against the truth may be, God's truths must be embraced. By embracing the truth, our minds can be transformed, and negative thoughts can be overcome.

When we have negative thoughts, they must be confronted with God's truths. If we find ourselves saying, "I've made too many mistakes" or "I'm such a failure," we should replace these thoughts with the truth. For the Scripture says God's love endures forever and he stands ready to forgive. This is seen in 1 Chr 16:34, "Give thanks to the LORD, for he is good; his love endures forever." And in Ps 86:5, "You, Lord, are forgiving and good, abounding in love to all who call to you."

Understanding the truth helps reduce negative thoughts. So, we must always embrace the truth with conscious effort.

Our Thoughts Influence Our Feelings

We aren't helpless against doubt and defeating thoughts. That's because God has given his truths to strengthen our minds. Negative thoughts can range from "I'm worthless!" to "God's unfair!"

to anything in between. But the key to happiness is stopping these negative thoughts before they start affecting our lives. And being aware of our thoughts is the first step toward understanding our emotions and achieving happiness.

Since thoughts influence emotions, it's necessary to know what we think, especially when we are trying to understand an emotional experience. When we become aware of feelings like anxiety, anger, or sadness we must look for the thoughts causing these feelings. We must recognize that doubtful and defeating thoughts cause these negative emotions.

But God's truths can refocus our minds and bring peace. That's because our mind is renewed when we surrender to God and embrace his truths. When we embrace his truths, our minds are changed from an old way of thinking to a new, spiritual way.

This tells us that negative thinking and unhappiness can be changed. But this change can only occur as we surrender to God's way. Even though this process may take time, our thoughts can start to reflect his truths today. And this is the path we must take if we are to obtain satisfaction in life.

Our thoughts change the way we feel. That means, when we have negative thoughts, we will have negative emotions. If we are convinced that bad circumstances await us in the future, we will become overwhelmed with worry. And if we assume our circumstances will bring us harm in some way, then we will feel fear. In each case, these thoughts lead us to doubt God's faithfulness and leave us discouraged.

Truly, fear and worry are common emotions. But we must turn to God for comfort regardless of how we feel.

The Source of Our Troubles, Wrong Beliefs

God exposes the source of our troubles when he searches our hearts. These issues may be hidden from us at first, but in time he shows us what we need to know. Often, the root of our troubles is wrong beliefs about God and ourselves. But only God's truths can set the mind free.

The way we find happiness is to resolve these issues once God has revealed them. He must reveal his truths because we can't fully comprehend his ways on our own. Fortunately, God desires to show his wisdom so we can experience lasting change. And when we know his truths, we will have joy and happiness.

But, sometimes, instead of embracing God's ways in faith, we reluctantly travel his path. Often, we are unwilling to follow him because we have developed wrong beliefs. Not only do we have wrong beliefs, but we also have our doubts.

Many times, these wrong beliefs go unquestioned and, over time, become like truths in our minds. But for us to willingly follow God, we must let go of these wrong beliefs that suggest his ways are imperfect.

Reflections on Our Emotions

Thoughts change emotions. But it seems that our feelings don't always reflect what we know is true. That's because all of us have experienced discouragement or anxiety even after we've embraced truths in Scripture.

In fact, it's common for us to know God's word, but then not feel the impact of his truths. But if we continue to focus on Scripture, feelings of discouragement and anxiety eventually fade. And as God helps us understand his word, emotions will start to align with what we know is true.

Emotions do not always portray a clear picture of the truth. Fear is a great example of this. We've all been afraid of something and later discovered that there wasn't a real reason to feel distressed. Even though there wasn't a real danger, we still experienced genuine fear.

In these situations, fear existed only in our thoughts and emotions. This demonstrates why emotions aren't a good representation of reality. That's because our emotions can be deceptive as they show us a reality that can't always be trusted.

Worry or anxiety is another emotion that can be deceptive. Sometimes, we experience worry over things that aren't in our control. Trying to predict how life will unfold can only lead to disappointment and frustration. But if we don't entrust our future to God, feelings of fear and doubt will overwhelm us. We must realize our feelings of worry can't be trusted. Instead, we must trust in God's promises that say he has a plan for us, and it's for our good.

Identifying Thoughts Causing Emotions

Negative thoughts and doubt often cause us to feel negative emotions. But understanding how these thoughts and beliefs impact our emotions is not simple. However, if we can notice when these thoughts and beliefs start to affect us, we can use the truth to correct the process.

To find out what's causing us to have feelings of anger, fear, or worry, we can ask questions like "What thoughts am I having, right now, that's causing me to feel these emotions?" "What thoughts are supporting my emotions?" or "What are the reasons I am feeling these emotions?"

It may sound simple enough, but we really want to find the connection between our current thoughts and the emotions we are having. Once we identify that connection, the truth can be used to confront our current thoughts to change the way we feel.

We have more happiness when negative thoughts and doubt are not controlling our emotions. That means we don't have to be overwhelmed by feelings of sorrow, worry, or anger. In fact, once we know what negative thoughts are influencing our emotions, we can replace them with the truth of God's word.

We might have thoughts like "I will always be alone" or "nothing ever goes right for me" but God says, "I will never leave you or forsake you" and "I am working everything for your good!" When we confront inaccurate views with the truth, it leads to fulfillment and increases our happiness.

Even though it might not be possible to have thoughts that fully reflect God's truths, we are being refined every day. Thankfully, God is patient and pays attention to every detail of our lives.

Sure, it may seem like it's taking a long time, but soon the process will be completed. And until then, we must continue in faith. However, if we're not careful we can get worn down. But don't be discouraged, there is good news! God promised we can have fulfillment in the middle of it all. And although his process takes time, we can start experiencing happiness today.

New Interests Now That We Are Alive to God

Allowing negative thoughts to magnify our troubles leaves us feeling unsatisfied. The good news is we don't have to continue feeling this way. Our emotions will change when we stop focusing on temporary problems and personal weaknesses. This isn't to say we should ignore our difficulties.

Instead, we should focus on the fact that our lives are changing to reflect God's nature. And thankfully, he has provided grace to sustain us through every season. Yes, we will make mistakes, but the important thing is to always embrace truth and allow God to transform us.

According to God's word, we have already been drastically changed. Romans 8:10–11 says, "But if Christ is in you . . . the Spirit gives life because of righteousness. And if the Spirit of him who raised Jesus from the dead is living in you, he who raised Christ from the dead will also give life to your mortal bodies because of his Spirit who lives in you."

The Scripture tells us that we were "dead to God" in our former lives before we believed in Christ. That means we didn't know God, were self-willed, and had little concern for spiritual truths. Being "dead to God" also meant we didn't try to honor God or follow his will. But things have changed now that we have faith in Christ. Now that we're made alive by the Spirit, we have eternal interests and seek to honor God in all we do.

When we honor God, he provides everything we need for a fulfilled life. Although God provides what is needed, we must do our part. Our responsibility is to focus our thoughts on God's truths and surrender to his ways. This is the path that leads to greater satisfaction in life. Sometimes, it takes conscious effort to focus and surrender. But when we do, these things can change the way we feel.

Resting in God's Mercy and Peace

Proverbs 10:22 says, "The blessing of the LORD brings wealth, without painful toil for it." There is fulfillment when we know God has blessed our lives. But to have his favor we must be living in the truth.

However, this is not about earning something from God, but about him providing good things for his children. These good things are given when our main desire is to please him. Certainly, contentment is one of the many good things that comes from pleasing him. But if we only seek temporary pleasures, we will be left feeling unsatisfied.

A "blessed" life means God is considerate of our every need. And we know he will be faithful to his promises when his attention is turned toward us.

There are many types of blessings we receive as believers. But the most significant blessing that every believer receives is one of "rest." So, what does that mean exactly? We receive rest in Christ from all attempts at trying to earn God's favor and approval.

In Heb 4:10 we read, "For anyone who enters God's rest also rests from their works, just as God did from his." God called this rest "blessed." We see this referenced in Exod 20:11, "For in six days the LORD made the heavens and the earth, the sea, and all that is in them, but he rested on the seventh day. Therefore, the LORD blessed the Sabbath day and made it holy."

This rest has been promised to every believer and occurs when we stop depending on our own ability to earn God's love and mercy. For his love isn't earned but is steady and abundant. And even though we may not feel much rest right now, God has promised to ultimately give us peace and joy. By letting God have our concerns, we can all experience the blessings of his rest.

Sometimes, we feel discouraged when God's blessings are delayed. But when we get discouraged, we need to check our priorities. That's because what we focus on determines our happiness. We need to ask ourselves this question, "Is my priority to please God, or have I become focused on temporary pleasures?"

Even though worldly pleasures fight for our attention, we must remain focused on God. In fact, what holds our attention shapes our lives. So, when the truth holds our thoughts, it leads to joy and happiness. And as we allow God to shape us, our hearts learn to be content.

We must make the choice to turn our desires toward God and away from temporary pursuits. When we realize what an awesome privilege it is to be in relationship with God, our hearts will fill with love. Truly, this is a relationship that can bring joy and gladness into every area of our lives.

Chapter 2

God's Process to Help Us

COMPLETE KNOWLEDGE OF GOD is not given all at once, but over time we learn of his ways. For it's through the truth that we learn about him and are brought into a closer relationship. Our role is to seek truth and never turn away from the person it reveals.

God wants to show himself, but sometimes we can't see clearly. Because his nature is different than ours, he uses a process to help us fully understand his ways. So, to help us, God works through a process of trials and testing. That's because we learn of his faithfulness and start to trust in his strength in times when we are weak.

It is through this process we learn to release control of self-will and accept our call to obedience. When we surrender and obey, our relationship with God is strengthened. And as we give everything to him, our spiritual experience brings happiness and fulfillment.

But even though we surrender, it doesn't mean this process will be easy. In fact, this journey can be unpleasant at times. But the reason we travel this path is not because it's easy, but because he leads us and because we love him.

The Choice Is Ours to Make

We can choose to have joy or distress. And it's our beliefs that determine our experience. When we believe God's truths it contributes to our joy, but our doubts and distrust lead to distress. If we aren't careful, doubtful thinking can start interfering with our contentment. This is the reason why it's so important to seek after the truth. For the truth helps us see life the way it really exists.

Sometimes, we don't have a clear understanding of God or of ourselves because doubtful thinking has distorted the truth. This lack of clear knowledge hinders hope and trust. And without hope and trust, God's process that is intended to bring us joy only results in distress.

Changing Our Hearts to Look Like Christ

The need for us to become more like Christ is always present and can often feel overwhelming. It's tempting to delay facing these spiritual changes so we can avoid being pushed to our limits. But we make a mistake if we seek comfort above all else and yet hope to possess the virtues of Christ. While it makes sense to avoid situations that are tough, delaying spiritual change too long may result in a loss of joy.

We only find peace and fulfillment while moving forward through every changing season. Even though we may not understand the reason for change at times, each season serves a specific purpose.

In some seasons, our relationship with God is tested. That's when we experience trials and his silence. Other seasons, our devotion to Christ is tested with a call to surrender. But when we realize that everything in God's process is intended to bring us joy, facing our struggles becomes a little easier.

It takes courage to look within our hearts and ask God to make us like Christ. In fact, thinking about a greater devotion to Christ can produce anxious feelings, and that's normal. No one can be just like Jesus, but we can all reflect his nature. Sometimes, we fear that God will ask for a great sacrifice, like he did of Christ. And this certainly can be an overwhelming thought. However, we experience the greatest joy when we become more like Jesus.

The Struggle against the Past and Old Ways of Thinking

There's hope for every situation whether we're facing impossible circumstances or God has become silent. We have hope because God's process is intended to bring us joy and fulfillment. It brings encouragement when we know God intends blessings for us in every situation. But it's not always easy to believe that we can have joy in the middle of our circumstances.

Trying to believe that joy is possible despite our difficulties is hard because there are often competing views in our minds. One view is influenced by faith and the other view sees through the lens of doubt. This is essentially the renewed mind struggling against old ways of thinking. And the renewed mind is empowered by the Spirit, but old ways of thinking are strengthened by self-will.

We struggle with old ways of thinking for many reasons. One reason is past experiences seem to influence our faith more than what God says. In fact, we may have emotional wounds from our past that haven't healed, which helps explain why we have so much difficulty overcoming doubt. Even though past experiences have shaped who we are, we should be able to believe and trust what God is doing in our present moments.

It's important to recognize what God is doing in our "now" moments. That's because focusing on our past can keep us trapped if our mind isn't centered on God. Past experiences can leave wounds that will cause us to say things like "I've tried this all before, and nothing works for me!" But God wants to change the way we view his process. We must see our trials through the lens of faith and become grounded in his truths. Then we'll have hope and experience true joy.

Many times, we grow accustomed to the distrustful views formed from past experiences. That means we have accepted the negative beliefs that caused doubt to be a regular part of our lives.

But spiritual change can happen for anyone willing to place their trust in God.

God gives us all the ability to experience change, but it's usually not an overnight cure. In fact, real change and happiness occur through a process of growth where we begin to reflect the nature of Christ. Even though it may take time to remove old ways of thinking, all that's needed to experience change and growth is sincere trust in God.

Sincere Belief in the Truth

Since our understanding of the truth is constantly increasing, our growth never stops. As we draw close to God, we learn to embrace his magnificence and rulership. Having an accurate view of God's magnificence helps us willingly submit to his process. But willingness doesn't happen automatically. It takes humility and openness to look within the secret places of our hearts and find the ability to surrender all we have to God.

Beginning on a path toward change requires that we first understand some things about ourselves. To understand whether our beliefs about life are accurate, our beliefs must be questioned. Beliefs that haven't been questioned or confronted are often assumed to be true. But we should never let beliefs that are assumed to be true replace the actual truth. The reason assumptions shouldn't be relied upon is because assumptions are hardly ever centered on real facts. Instead, they're often based on our own biased opinions and emotions.

One belief that is often assumed to be true is that God's favor is earned. Based on this thinking, we would naturally assume that our routine devotions and good deeds give us his approval. But this isn't how God works. Sure, charity and routines are important. But God is really looking for faith and delights in our obedience.

Though this is a simplistic example, we do all sorts of things to earn God's favor. All with the hope that he will give his approval and send his blessings. The truth is God is not moved by our works; he is more impressed by the sincerity of our faith, whether it be great or small.

Sincere Faith Prepares the Heart

The journey of sincerity can seem like a lonely one, but God is with us to be our guide. We can start to feel empty once we let go of every belief that isn't grounded in the truth. But remember, God is just preparing our heart for what he's about to place inside. To receive what God intends to give, we must have a surrendered heart, which is the purest form of sincerity.

Sincerity develops when we freely choose to believe God at his word. Certainly, we are free to believe anything we want. But God invites us to embrace his truths. And his truths challenge us to be like Christ asking us to be more loving, forgiving, and accepting.

As we become more like Christ, God shows us the wrong beliefs that hinders our spiritual growth. For it's our beliefs that cause us to either endure God's process in hope or abandon his way in doubt. When we realize that his process helps us become like Christ, it brings us hope. And this hope gives us strength to face every trial.

The Spirit Living in Us Brings Contentment

Our lives look different when we truly surrender to God. And because we have Jesus in our heart, everything we do should reflect God's nature. The Scripture says we have been given life with Jesus. Colossians 3:1 says, "Since . . . you have been raised with Christ, set your hearts on things above, where Christ is, seated at the right hand of God."

Believers may express their faith in different ways, but one thing that's common to all is the Spirit of God within every heart. And if the Holy Spirit is allowed to guide us, we will experience true happiness. Many try to achieve contentment on their own but don't fully reach their goal. For without a relationship with God, a person cannot be truly content. But everyone who has God in their heart can live with joy and happiness no matter what circumstances they face.

Spirituality is an essential part of every believer's identity. And we should not take this for granted since it is the almighty God living in our hearts. It's true that God wanted to be close to us from the beginning of creation. So, when Adam sinned in the garden, God set his plan in motion to dwell in our hearts and be near us again.

Galatians 3:14 says, "He redeemed us in order that the blessing given to Abraham might come to the Gentiles through Christ Jesus, so that by faith we might receive the promise of the Spirit." This new life, which is a heart filled with the Spirit of God, is obtained through faith in Christ alone. For it cannot be earned. But sometimes, we lose sight of the Spirit's importance as he is often overshadowed by our efforts to find contentment on our own.

Living in the Spirit Changes Our Priorities

Joy, happiness, and contentment come from knowing God has drawn us close because of his mercy. So, by remembering God's mercies our love for him will be rekindled and we'll be inspired to rethink our priorities. And when truth is valued, our focus won't be on acquiring temporary comforts. Instead, we'll seek to be more like Jesus who showed us how to trust and follow God.

Because our lives have been touched by God, our worldly pursuits have ended. This means old ways of living are over now that Jesus has made a way for us to live free. Second Corinthians 5:17 says, "Therefore, if anyone is in Christ, the new creation has come: The old has gone, the new is here!" Following Christ means that we have the Spirit of God living in our hearts. And when the Spirit is living inside, he becomes the source for change and happiness.

Romans 8:11 says, "And if the Spirit of him who raised Jesus from the dead is living in you, he who raised Christ from the dead will also give life to your mortal bodies." Spiritual growth should be our highest priority, and we must allow God to bring continuous change to our lives. The reason it's important to focus on our spiritual growth is because we are happiest when we become like Christ.

Finding Comfort and Encouragement in God

It's exciting to know that we have the same Spirit in our hearts that raised Jesus from the dead. This means that nothing we face will be impossible for God. And not only can God do the impossible, but we have confidence that he will be with us during our troubles. This truth offers us hope when we face difficulties. So, we must encourage ourselves to keep waiting on God's promises and keep praying for answers.

As believers we will face hardships and our determination will be tested, but God is faithful to comfort and support his people through the tough times. So, when times get tough, remember, God is faithful and will not let us down!

God promised to be with us in the middle of our trials and help us overcome by his strength. Even when he seems silent, he is still working out our deliverance. No matter what circumstance we face, God can bring peace and joy to our hearts if we will only trust him. For if we trust him when he is silent, he will make a way.

When God gives peace and joy it reminds us that our struggles are only temporary. For he gives a peace that is beyond circumstances and this connects us to our eternal hope. However, this doesn't mean that our trials are insignificant, in fact they're very important. But it helps us stay focused on what awaits in the future.

We have been called to an eternal glory in Christ and this gives us comfort when facing difficulties. Sometimes, we lose sight of these promises and get discouraged when our troubles become overwhelming. However, God knows our concerns and will always provide encouragement and strength at just the right time.

Our Joy Transcends Every Circumstance

Hope comes from embracing the truth of God's faithfulness. This means we recognize that he is committed to us in times of trouble. Focusing on God's ability to get us through tough times helps us have a greater understanding of his love and faithfulness.

When our thoughts are centered on him, we find the confidence and encouragement needed to face trials. We must remind ourselves that challenges are not intended to overwhelm us. Instead, he wants us to learn how to trust him so he can strengthen and comfort us through our trials.

God promised to provide everything we need for a fulfilling life. And according to the Scripture, every true blessing is given to us because we have a relationship with Christ. Ephesians 1:3 says, "Praise be to the God and Father of our Lord Jesus Christ, who has blessed us in the heavenly realms with every spiritual blessing in Christ."

We are blessed even when facing trials. That's because the Spirit provides his favor and helps us endure. Even though God doesn't deliver us from certain hardships, he still gives us the strength we need to persevere.

No matter what we might think, we are never alone, especially not in our darkest hour. We can find comfort knowing that God will provide what we need to get us through every trial. Embracing these truths will bring us encouragement and lead to more happiness.

Happiness occurs when we look beyond our trials to fully embrace the eternal rewards that are in God. We may look at our situation and think there's no reason to be content. But an understanding of the truth tells us that spiritual blessings, like peace, are received through Christ alone.

We must know that happiness doesn't come directly from our current circumstances. Instead, a divine source provides joy that transcends every situation. Knowing our happiness is based on God's faithfulness changes our perspective on trials and brings us closer to fulfillment in life.

Chapter 3

Acknowledging God's Goodwill

FIRST TIMOTHY 6:6 SAYS, "Godliness with contentment is great gain." This tells us that fulfillment and happiness flow from an obedient life. We are blessed when we accept and follow God's sovereign will. But following God's will can be scary at times because we don't always know what's going to happen next. Is this the right opportunity? Is this the right decision? Is this the right time?

When God's path leads into the unknown, he sometimes remains painfully silent. And that's when doubtful thoughts begin to surface. But the question is, "Will we trust God enough to follow him into the unknown?"

How we respond to God's unknowable ways determines our satisfaction in life. If we respond in faith we'll develop courage, but if we choose to doubt, we'll be full of fear. However, fear does not have to fill our hearts. That's because God has made a way for us to rest from our worries.

There's a sense of peace once we realize God is high above our circumstances. Since he's above our troubles, we must learn to embrace his will and not demand to have our own way. This means we stop wrestling for control. When God is allowed to be our God, we find rest from fear and doubt. There's no need to worry. And because we are in his hands, he will bring us safely through the unknowns in life.

God has eternity in sight and knows what's best for us. Of course, we can't help but ask, "How can the difficult things be what's best for me?" Well, they can, because God has a different point of view. He wants to bring eternal fulfillment whereas we seek temporary satisfaction. This means, if eternal good can come from momentary pain, God will allow the pain.

We see these principles throughout Scripture where people experienced suffering for the opportunity of an eternal reward. Even Jesus himself suffered and was glorified. Now he is in heaven where he remains today, awaiting his kingdom.

God wants us to know that we can trust him to do what's right. But he wants us to let go of control. This can be tough at times, but we must have confidence that he is able to handle any situation.

No matter what we face, our situation is never too difficult for God. He is neither intimidated nor confused by our problems. Even though uncertainty may fill our hearts, God knows exactly what he's doing. Just because we don't know what he's up to doesn't mean there isn't a divine plan.

It's also encouraging to know God loves us and wants to carry our worries and fears. It says in 1 Pet 5:7, "Cast all your anxiety on him because he cares for you."

Divine Ability to Overcome Trials

Doubting whether our current experiences reflect God's goodness causes distrust to fill our hearts. In fact, a skeptical perspective will erode our faith in God. And as our faith fades, our thoughts become less focused on the truth. If these thoughts and doubts continue, our confidence and joy will dwindle.

We've all experienced doubt at some point in our lives. But God doesn't want us to stay hopeless. In fact, God desires that we live with love and boldness. In 2 Tim 1:7 we read, "For the Spirit God gave us does not make us timid, but gives us power, love and self-discipline."

Having an eternal perspective helps us to be brave when we're facing challenges. We can be confident when going through difficulties because we know God is with us. Not only are we confident because God's with us, but we also have boldness because we understand that our trials serve a greater eternal purpose. Just knowing God is behind-the-scenes accomplishing something for our eternal good brings encouragement and leads to greater satisfaction in life.

It's comforting to know that God doesn't want us to be defeated by our problems. His desire is that we live with strength. That means we don't have to be overwhelmed with doubt, negative thoughts, or unstable emotions. So, we can know, if God wants us to have strength, then it will be freely given. The only thing we need to do is receive his gift.

Strength through Weakness

Truly, we were given the ability to thrive when we became believers. In fact, when we accepted Christ and received the Spirit, we also received the power to overcome adversity. Every believer can overcome challenges through the Spirit. However, the way we overcome our troubles may look different than what we expect.

Of course, in every situation, we need God's strength to conquer our adversity. But for God to show his strength, he often leads us down paths that reveal our weaknesses. In other words, God doesn't correct all our flaws, but shows his strength despite our imperfections.

It seems ironic that to overcome our trials, we must learn to embrace our weaknesses. But that's God's way. Even though our weaknesses surface during trials, God still considers us strong when we place our faith and trust in him.

God knows it's difficult for us to embrace our limitations. And the reason it's difficult is because we often learn of our weaknesses by encountering adversity. Sometimes, when we face troubles, it feels like our discomfort is more than we can handle. But we can be assured that God will provide a way through the distress.

Certainly, confronting challenges head-on and working through discomfort takes courage. But it ultimately leads to freedom. Thankfully, we don't have to do this alone. That's because God will help us confront our doubts and fears so we can live in faith. Even though living in faith doesn't always make sense, it's what helps us find lasting change.

Not Alone, Not Abandoned

Even though we often feel alone, God does not expect us to overcome by our own power. One of our greatest challenges is feeling abandoned when we face adversity. Sometimes, it is merely our doubt and despair that lead us into these barren lands.

We start to isolate ourselves from God's presence and even begin to resist his comfort. When we feel like this, we can find comfort knowing that God desires to meet us in these lonely places. Deuteronomy 31:6 says, "Be strong and courageous. Do not be afraid or terrified . . . for the LORD your God goes with you; he will never leave you nor forsake you."

It is during the darkest days that we often feel abandoned. But be encouraged because the "dark times" are God's meeting place. A place where he brings us closer to himself. In times of hardship, we are drawn together so he can reveal his strength.

Though we may feel alone, we are not alone. In fact, he is bringing us close. And God is known for doing amazing things when he is close.

Peace Because of God's Goodness

We experience lasting change when we are content with God's work in our lives. For it's not possible to find true contentment in temporary pleasures. But we can have peace when we trust in God.

It says in Isa 26:3, "You will keep in perfect peace those whose minds are steadfast, because they trust in you." Focusing our thoughts on God's truths gives us strength. Though we are not guaranteed an escape from our troubles, God has promised to give us peace and fulfillment.

When we focus on God's goodness, we can endure trials with joy. That's because we know God will give us strength no matter what we face. In fact, God will use these situations for our eternal good, but we must continue to trust him.

It's easy to be discouraged when our future appears dark and hopeless. But rather than being discouraged, we should start expecting God's favor in every circumstance. This doesn't mean everything will be comfortable. Instead, it means God will use our circumstances for our eternal good.

We might not be glad when trials come our way, but these challenges do help us grow. That's because adversity strengthens our minds and refines our character. Certainly, trials don't always feel like a good thing, but growth happens when limits are tested.

However, leaving God's process delays his plan. Although it doesn't stop his plan, it does slow us from reaching what he intends for our lives. But no matter how long the process takes, God ensures we will reach our destiny if we trust him. He will finish his work!

This promise even accounts for when we delay his work by trying to avoid discomfort. But leaving trials isn't the correct response to our troubles. For it is during trials when our limits are appropriately stretched.

The Reason for the Stretching

Ironically, being stretched is a good thing. That's because adversity helps us learn something about ourselves. It can uncover issues causing doubt and distrust. And by confronting these issues with the truth, we learn to have more happiness and contentment.

In fact, trials help us discover the reasons why we feel insecure, abandoned, or unloved. These basic beliefs work in the background and continue to affect us even when the trial itself is over. Interestingly, these beliefs form in various ways. Issues like this can stem from past experiences. Often, we are unaware of the reasons for our beliefs, but trials help us realize there are deeper issues we need to address.

When doubts surface, we can confront them with the truth. And if we let God, he will clear negative thoughts and doubts from our minds. However, this process might make us uncomfortable. That's because healing only occurs when the testing process is allowed to run its full course.

So, by allowing God to test our limits he can build character and make us complete. James 1:2–4 says, "Consider it pure joy, my brothers and sisters, whenever you face trials of many kinds, because you know that the testing of your faith produces perseverance. Let perseverance finish its work so that you may be mature and complete, not lacking anything." God wants us to be complete and whole, which is only accomplished in Christ. It might be difficult to believe that our troubles make us more like Jesus, but they do if we stay in faith.

It helps to remember that trials are always intended to bring eternal blessings and never to cause harm. So, even when we are overwhelmed by challenges, we must remember these momentary difficulties are designed with our well-being in mind. That's why we are encouraged to stay in the testing process and never abandon God's plan.

Wrong Opinions of God and Ourselves

Because we accepted Jesus as our Savior, the Spirit now helps us reflect Christ's nature. And since we can please God only by faith in Christ, we should acknowledge the inadequacy of our own efforts.

But even though we are imperfect, our inadequacies and flaws must not prevent us from finding fulfillment in God. In other words, contentment should not be based on our progress or abilities but rather on God's faithfulness.

A full understanding of God might not be possible in this life. Many times, what we know about him is wrong and unreliable. We can start to believe that God is not fair or that he doesn't do what's best for us. These beliefs form because our views are based on partial truths about his nature. We might think since God is fair, everyone should prosper in the same way. Or because he is good, we should always expect comfort.

These are obvious misrepresentations of the truth. But the truth is we all prosper according to God's will, and both comfort and correction come from his hands. So, the actual truth should determine what we believe, not our own misunderstandings.

Not only do we have misunderstandings about God's nature and goodwill, but we also have inaccurate opinions of ourselves. It becomes a problem when we believe things like "God couldn't love someone like me" or "I'm just not that important to him." These ideas question our worth and are not supported by the truth.

Again, this shows why we can't rely on our own understanding.

Staying Connected with the Truth

Embracing God's truths as the final authority builds character and leads to contentment. But this contentment only comes when we hold on to the truth. In other words, we are to be so connected to God's principles that they become the main influence of our thoughts and emotions.

Of course, Christ is the ultimate truth. And without love and devotion to him we can't have peace. Jesus said in John 15:5, "I am the vine; you are the branches. If you remain in me and I in you, you will bear much fruit; apart from me you can do nothing." Trying to pursue happiness and fulfillment without Jesus will leave us incomplete.

Staying connected to Christ allows spiritual character to be formed. Not only will our attitudes and behaviors look more like Jesus, but our thoughts will also be changed. However, when we don't challenge our thoughts with the truth, it leads to wrong beliefs about God.

But just because we believe something is true in our minds doesn't make it automatically true. We must accept the fact that our thoughts are not always right. When we acknowledge this, we can avoid being blinded by our own beliefs.

Godly Virtues Developed by the Spirit

Christlikeness is formed through a refining process. For there's no other way to attain these qualities except by following in the footsteps of Jesus. Just as Jesus submitted to God's rulership and was tested, likewise we are to endure the refining process in faith.

If we want the rewards of a spiritual life, we must follow Christ's example. Just like the branch is to the vine, likewise we can't possess these holy attributes separate from the Spirit's work through Christ. Sure, we may be able to attain some level of morality and self-control on our own, but Christlikeness can't be duplicated without the Holy Spirit. And the Spirit accomplishes his work through the refining process.

Striving for self-control and mastery is necessary, but these pursuits fall short when the Spirit's work is not embraced. It's not that we should disregard discipline and morality, but our efforts must be accomplished through God's strength.

We discover strength and self-control by surrendering to God. When we surrender, godly virtues develop in our lives. This means the Spirit can work in our lives to develop qualities only he can create. Galatians 5:22–23 says, "The fruit of the Spirit is love, joy, peace, forbearance, kindness, goodness, faithfulness, gentleness and self-control."

When we desire to have what God offers, we experience fulfillment and blessing. Jesus said in Matt 5:6, "Blessed are those who hunger and thirst for righteousness, for they will be filled."

Fulfillment comes from living in the Spirit. For it is the Spirit who helps us be more like Christ. And when the Spirit makes us like Christ, we find comfort despite our difficulties. And because we are being changed, feelings of fear, worry, and anger fade. But we shouldn't allow emotions to interfere with the Spirit's work. Instead, we must follow God regardless of how we feel.

We find comfort and contentment when we allow God's truths to shape our minds. Any distress we experience will diminish. This is because his truths prevent us from being trapped by negative feelings, freeing us from despair, hopelessness, and worry.

When we put God first, we will be changed by his truths. And this leads to greater happiness and contentment.

Growth from Our Troubles

Our comfort is not the only thing that matters. While it is important to be free from troubles, embracing God's process is more important. That's because we experience significant growth during these challenging times. We also gain a better understanding of God's ways and are drawn closer to him when we face difficulties.

When we look at our situation from an eternal perspective, we see that life is more about relying on him than having ease from our troubles. That means in some ways our journey of faith is more important than the deliverance we seek.

Sometimes, we seek immediate relief from our burdens, but instead God gives us strength to endure. We must understand he doesn't allow hardships simply because he's cruel. Rather, God knows we can't grow into our destiny without experiencing some adversity. Certainly, he cares about our troubles, but he is more interested in us growing in Christ.

God shows he cares for us by revealing himself in times of weakness. But to see him, we must surrender our strength and become vulnerable. And to surrender everything, our love for him must overshadow any discomfort. This means we stop trying to escape trials but enter them with a passion for God.

Watch How We Grow

Our love for him helps us grow through challenges. But growth happens only when our trust remains in him.

Our growth is a unique process, and it can't be rushed. Surely, our growth can be hindered and slowed, but embracing truth keeps us on course. Even though growth isn't always predictable, we already know what it looks like in the end. For us, we will eventually reflect the full nature of Christ. But how this process unfolds is another one of God's mysteries.

In the beginning, new growth is small and imperfect, but when it's completely grown, it becomes something magnificent. We see this throughout nature.

Have you ever tried to watch a flower bloom? You wait day after day, through all types of weather. You don't see much growth, but soon you start to notice little buds. Then, suddenly, at the right time, the flower begins to blossom. This is how it is for us as we develop. We grow in small ways to please God and delight his eye alone. We might not see our own growth, but he does. And then, at the right time, the nature of Christ breaks forth and shines through our lives.

Though we may not see much growth right now, our lives will eventually bloom. Regardless of how it appears, we are assured that God is behind-the-scenes working to bring about change and restoration.

Even nature tells us that growth occurs over time. Likewise, God has a pace at which we grow. We can't grow faster than he intends, but we must be careful not to slow the Spirit's work. But when we follow the Spirit's guidance, our growth begins to flourish.

Starting with Small Faith

We flourish when we embrace situations that help us grow. This means we do not run or shy away from difficult or challenging experiences. Even though some challenges seem impossible to endure, God gives us the strength to make it through.

The good news is we already have what it takes to overcome our trials. During difficult times, what we need is faith to help us face our troubles. It doesn't take great faith. All we need is simple, sincere reliance on God. And when we depend on God in faith, he will help us grow from our challenges.

It is not the amount of faith but the sincerity that makes the difference. As we depend on God, he will perform amazing works in our lives.

Jesus said if we had just a little faith, compared to the size of a mustard seed, we would see great things. We see this in Matt 17:20, "Truly I tell you, if you have faith as small as a mustard seed, you can say to this mountain, 'Move from here to there,' and it will move. Nothing will be impossible for you."

A seed has small beginnings and later becomes something magnificent. Likewise, our simple, sincere trust can be transformed into great strength through God's power.

The Truth Brings Wisdom

God wants each of us to understand his ways. All we need to do is ask and he will give the wisdom and knowledge we need to learn his truths.

We read in Col 1:9–10, "We continually ask God to fill you with the knowledge of his will through all the wisdom and understanding that the Spirit gives so that you may live a life worthy of the Lord and please him in every way: bearing fruit in every good work, growing in the knowledge of God."

It's God's truths alone that effectively change us. But these changes can only happen when we embrace him. So, our hearts must always be ready to follow the truth.

God makes us aware of these truths through his word. For this is how we gain wisdom, get understanding, and ultimately experience change. Second Timothy 3:16–17 says, "All Scripture is God-breathed and is useful for teaching, rebuking, correcting and training in righteousness, so that the servant of God may be thoroughly equipped for every good work."

God's truths bring strength when times are tough. That's because the truth renews our thoughts and helps us understand who God is. Once we know the truth, it brings the encouragement and strength we need for the journey.

This knowledge helps us have hope in our adversity. Sometimes, all we need is a little hope. And we have hope because the truth says God has blessed us in every circumstance.

God watches over us carefully to ensure we experience his goodness. The truth is our trials are not for his benefit. Instead, we endure adversity for our good. For when we endure trials faithfully and follow his path it leads to our fulfillment.

The Truth Helps Us Trust God

God's truths determine our standard for living. However, God's principles do not exist simply to give us an example of moral behavior. They are meant to show us how to reflect his character of holiness and righteousness.

We already stand before God in righteousness because our faith is in Christ. But even though we have this righteousness doesn't mean we can bypass God's refining process. That means we must let him finish what he started. Surely, he wants to complete his work, but it is up to us to allow his plan to unfold.

For us to trust as we should, the doubt in our hearts must be rooted out. God often accomplishes this by placing us in situations that require us to depend on him. As he leads us down paths of adversity, we learn to trust and have confidence by focusing on his faithfulness. And when our focus is on God, trust develops despite the challenges we face.

Trials can either weaken or strengthen our faith. Trials have weakened our faith if we are left questioning God's truths and doubting his promises. However, if we endure trials and turn to his truths for hope, our faith will be strengthened.

Trials then become opportunities to test our faith and develop greater dependence on God. In times of hardship, we must accept God's ways and allow our thinking to be shaped by his truths. As we embrace his truths and apply them to our lives, we will find hope and encouragement.

Chapter 4

Happiness in God's Presence

GOD GIVES FAVOR TO his people, but that's not why we serve him. We serve him because we love him. And even though he blesses us, we shouldn't neglect our relationship with him just to receive his gifts. Instead, we must seek his heart, not the things he provides. For if we pursue blessings alone, we won't be satisfied, but if we seek his heart, it will lead to true fulfillment.

In the Scripture, we are described as a tree that has been planted by peaceful waters. Psalm 1:1–3 says,

> Blessed is the one who does not walk in step with the wicked or stand in the way that sinners take or sit in the company of mockers, but whose delight is in the law of the LORD, and who meditates on his law day and night. That person is like a tree planted by streams of water, which yields its fruit in season and whose leaf does not wither—whatever they do prospers.

Like the tree planted by a stream, we also have access to a life sustaining, heavenly resource. Without this connection to a heavenly resource, our fruit and spiritual virtue fade. But we don't have to worry about our spiritual connection fading because Jesus has given us complete access to the true source of life. And even though spiritual blessings are important, this connection with God must be our highest priority.

Focusing on Our Relationship with God

Happiness and fulfillment are achieved by having a close relationship with God. However, this relationship doesn't work if it's only one-sided. In other words, we have a role to play. And our role is to seek after God's heart.

God wants to be near us, and likewise, we should want to be near him. And although he came to us first, our relationship grows when we return our affection.

When God is drawing us close, every situation becomes an opportunity for growth, a chance to reflect Christ's nature. So, this means our focus should be on God and not on our own problems.

When our mind is set on eternal matters, we experience divine flow in the Spirit. And like a tree planted by peaceful waters, this divine flow is always available to us. We experience this flow only when we deepen our relationship with God and stay in the refining process.

So, if we want greater encounters with God, know that he will be faithful to reveal himself.

Our View of the Kingdom

God has called us unto salvation and now offers an invitation to a more devoted relationship. Notice, it's God who is calling us into a closer walk with Jesus, and it's his voice we hear. John 6:44 says, "No one can come to me unless the Father who sent me draws them."

This means God draws us close and we are to respond with total surrender. It's normal to fear that God will require more of us as we enter deeper levels of devotion. Yes, he will ask us to give more of ourselves as we draw near. But even if we are asked to make sacrifices, he offers to exchange our discomfort for eternal rewards.

There's no need to worry.

We won't be disappointed if we surrender everything for God.

Consider the parable of the man who made it his business to find precious pearls (Matt 13:45–46). This man's business depended on his ability to recognize quality jewels. One day he found a pearl so valuable, he sold everything he had to purchase this single gem alone. To him, this one pearl was more precious than all his possessions.

This is how we should view God's kingdom. What we have in Christ is far more valuable than any possession we could possibly own. It's only when we abandon all for God and draw close to him that we find true happiness and peace.

A Desire to Be with Us from the Beginning

God is really the one pursuing us although it can seem like we have been doing all the searching. Remember, God came looking for us even before we knew him. And as a result, we are in a relationship with him today because he first reached out to us in love.

First John 4:19 says, "We love because he first loved us." This means God had us on his mind from the beginning and has always wanted to be close. And because of his love, everything has already been done to make it possible for him to dwell among his people.

Throughout Scripture we find evidence of God's desire to live among believers. When God raised up the children of Israel, he wanted the nations around them to know that his people were different. They were indeed unique, but what set them apart was his presence in their lives.

We see how God's presence was revealed through Moses's tabernacle (Exod 40:34–35) and later manifested in Solomon's temple (2 Chr 7:1–3). And today, we have become the sanctuary for God's presence.

Now, God chooses to reveal himself inside our hearts and minds. We read in 2 Cor 6:16, "For we are the temple of the living God. As God has said: 'I will live with them and walk among them, and I will be their God, and they will be my people.'"

Just as God's presence was manifest in Old Testament structures, he intends to make himself fully known today. He wants us to understand the mysteries of his person. But we don't have to wait around for visions and dreams to discover him. Instead, we can observe his nature and his ways right now.

However, what we know of him often comes through revealed truths found in Scripture. And when we embrace these truths, our knowledge and understanding of him increases.

Many times, we can't hear God's spoken truth because our worries have become too great. Problems and difficulties often make it difficult to find out what he is saying. But no matter what we face, it's important to keep listening. And sometimes, if we listen close enough, we will hear him.

Drawing Close to a Holy God

God's love was expressed to us through Jesus, and it's through Jesus we find mercy and forgiveness. Realizing how much we have been forgiven helps us serve God with passion. We see this in Luke 7:40–47, "Now which of them will love him more . . . the one who had the bigger debt forgiven . . . whoever has been forgiven little loves little."

Our love grows when we realize Jesus paid an impossible debt so we could receive a priceless reward. When we are grateful for God's forgiveness, it won't matter what he asks of us because every sacrifice is worth it when it brings us closer to him.

Since our relationship has been restored with God, our hearts can now draw close. And as we draw close, we start to understand him more. But even though he loves us, he is still holy.

In the Old Testament, the Scripture tells us, God required the tabernacle and temple to be cleansed and dedicated for his service. Only then would his presence show up and fill these places. Cleansing and dedication were done because God is holy, and it's against his nature to dwell in defiled places.

God's purity was also revealed at other times in the Scripture. And these appearances often caused unique reactions as well. On one occasion, the writer of the book of Revelation said that his life

34

seemed to leave his body. Revelation 1:17 says, "When I saw him, I fell at his feet as though dead."

God is holy and he fills eternity with his glory. However, only a glimpse of these attributes can be seen in this life. But because we are in a fallen state, we are mostly aware of our own shortcomings.

Even though his righteousness is far above our own, he still chooses to draw us near. Any moral qualities we believe we possess are eclipsed by his righteousness. And this truth makes us aware of the great gap between his holiness and our human nature. But instead of feeling discouraged, this should spark a strong desire to be pure like our heavenly Father. It's this desire that gives us motivation to change and deepen our relationship.

Certainly, God's holiness is above our own. But thankfully there is a way to obtain righteousness, and that is by faith in Christ.

Seeing the difference between God's nature and our own can inspire change. But it can be unclear sometimes which area in our lives needs to change first. That's because only God can open our eyes to the real issues causing us problems. And when he shows up, he reveals the thoughts and beliefs that do not align with the truth.

Since it is not possible to remain the same in his presence, old ways of thinking start to fade, and the process of change begins. So, by showing us the root of our problems, we can experience lasting change from the inside out.

Remaining Humble to Receive Instruction

The good news is we don't have to hold on to the ideas not grounded in God's truths. That's because they do not result in joy or peace. For the thoughts that cause us to doubt disappear in his presence. Because when we are close, he makes it clear we are loved and belong in his kingdom. Experiencing God's love like this motivates us to embrace his process no matter how difficult it may be.

To experience change, we must not turn away from the truth. Sure, there will be times when we find the truth offensive, unpleasant, and difficult to accept. But if we choose not to reject the truth, God will help us receive his instruction. That's why we must always stay prepared to receive the truth by remaining humble and sincere. Because when we are in this state of humility, we are easily guided by the truth.

There are difficult truths we must learn, but keeping a humble heart makes it easier to understand God's ways. Although his ways can be difficult to understand at times, we are never left to face tough issues alone. That's because God has promised to be with us in every circumstance.

Even now, he is faithfully preparing our hearts to receive his truths by removing self-will. Sometimes, God waits to reveal himself until we have been humbled and broken by circumstances. He does this so we can see him clearly. But there's no need to worry, God has promised to be close to us during these times. It says in Ps 34:18, "The LORD is close to the brokenhearted and saves those who are crushed in spirit."

No Problem Accepting the Truth

Being able to accept the truth is an important part of attaining satisfaction in life. For it's not possible to be happy if we disagree with God. And we cannot have peace if there's conflict within us over the truth.

These conflicts come in many forms, but they always position our will against God's. For example, the truth asks us to love unconditionally, but because of past hurts, we may hold onto resentments instead. Another example might be that we feel the need to hold on to temporary comforts, but the truth instructs us to abandon everything for Christ. All these things place us at odds with the truth and must be resolved so we can have real contentment.

Living conflicted over the truth hinders the flow of God's Spirit. And when the Spirit's work is hindered, our growth is slowed. However, it doesn't mean we are less of a believer for having dilemmas with the truth. Even though God's plan can be difficult to follow at times, in the end, it always yields life.

But if we want the Spirit to be involved in our lives, we must choose to side with the truth. And when we decide to embrace the truth at any cost, the Spirit is freed to move in our situation.

The Dilemma of God's Way

There is a difference between God's ways and our ways. And the Scripture gives many examples of this.

During Jesus's ministry, he showed that common ideas about how to live for God were not always right. This meant Jesus placed his listeners in a dilemma. Their dilemma was whether they should listen to Jesus's words or hold on to what they have always believed. They had to make a choice. Listeners should've been able to recognize that Jesus's words were truth. But even those that sided with the truth often found his words tough, yet somehow full of life.

Certainly, Jesus's messages conveyed hope. However, these messages didn't follow the common understanding of his day. Jesus taught that we should compare our lives to God's truths before evaluating others and allow God alone to judge in righteousness (Matt 7:1). That we should get more assurance from our trust in God than from our ability to earn his favor (Mark 10:24–25). And that the love we have for others is to resemble God's selfless compassion for all people (Luke 10:30–37).

Even though Jesus's messages were often difficult to receive, his words came from God. So, when we surrender to God and embrace his word, conflicts over the truth are removed, confusion fades, and our confidence is restored.

Bringing God Closer to Our Broken Heart

Our responsibility is turning toward God and embracing all he reveals. This means we fully accept his truths with all our heart, even when it's difficult. Sure, negative thoughts and doubts will surface when we face challenges. Which often leaves us feeling hurt and brokenhearted. But we are assured God will protect us from harm.

Knowing there isn't a foreseeable end to our challenges can leave us feeling crushed. But we don't have to fear. God tells us we are overcomers even when we feel weak. But overcoming doesn't mean we have to depend on our abilities alone.

Instead, it means we recognize nothing can be done without God's help. For only God can bring us through trials and help us find eternal meaning in our experiences. And even though faith and trust in God don't make adversity easy, they do bring him closer to our broken heart.

God can be trusted to get us through hard times and will remain faithful when we have our doubts. But if we want to find peace and happiness, we must embrace these truths. And when we do, it will renew our confidence in him.

Wrestling with the Truth

There are many reasons we struggle to embrace a truth once it is revealed. One reason is past offenses make it difficult to embrace what God is saying. Instead of embracing truths with faith and trust, we hide behind pain and resentment. Another reason is we often have hurt feelings and anger toward God. We think he hasn't been considerate of our needs when carrying out his plans and feel mistreated.

Regardless of the cause for our reluctance, it seems perfectly reasonable to wrestle with God's words. Now, we might be saying, "Surely, sincere believers do not wrestle with God's words?" Yes, we do. And that's exactly what we do when we resist God's invitation to love more sincerely, forgive more genuinely, and commit more completely.

It's important to question thoughts that suggest we have been wronged, overlooked, or undervalued by God. Turning our focus away from God's compassion and onto our own comfort causes us to develop this kind of thinking. If we are to live a fulfilled life, there needs to be a shift in our mindset. We need to view our circumstances through an eternal lens and assess whether our thoughts align with the truth. Then we can allow the truth to bring balance to our emotions.

We also need to understand why embracing God's truths is so challenging. We do this by identifying the beliefs behind our feelings. When we understand what holds us back, we can confront these ideas with the truth.

Often, it's wrong beliefs that keep us from embracing the truth. In other words, we can't fully trust God, if we believe he's being unfair or is withholding favor. Or we can't fully rely on him if we think he will not meet our needs. But when we acknowledge God's ways and turn toward him with an open heart, our doubts will start to fade, and our confidence will be restored. Then we can say our trust is in God alone!

Thoughts Reflect What's in Our Hearts

Faith-inspired thoughts affect what we speak. Focusing our minds on God's truths helps us express words of faith. But if our thoughts are negative, we won't have anything to say that can inspire hope. The Spirit wants to strengthen us, but if we just focus on our hurts and disappointments, challenges will only lead us to doubt and complain.

Truly, our words reflect what is in our hearts. And hearts full of spiritual life declare God's truths. However, wounded hearts mostly complain of their struggle.

Words, in themselves, are not necessarily the problem, but what overflows out of our hearts is of greater concern. When we have fully embraced God's truths, our words come from a place of trust, hope, and faith. But if we withdraw from him, we will speak from offense, bitterness, and doubt.

The issue is not with specific expressions of language but in the condition of our heart. Luke 6:45 says, "A good man brings good things out of the good stored up in his heart, and an evil man brings evil things out of the evil stored up in his heart. For the mouth speaks what the heart is full of."

How Good Qualities Form

Embracing God's ways helps good qualities develop in our hearts. However, developing good virtue in our hearts doesn't happen automatically. In fact, God has a unique way of forming spiritual character in our lives. He develops character through a divine process of purging and refinement that cannot be bypassed. Trying to avoid or resist this work only results in slowed progress.

Sometimes, we try to bypass or resist God's refining process because we don't want our weaknesses to be confronted. But despite our best efforts to escape, God still wants us to have an abundant life filled with joy.

However, he knows for us to have an abundant life we'll have to go through some trials. Unfortunately, there is no other way to obtain an abundant life if we want lasting happiness. And the only way to have true fulfillment is by turning our hearts toward God and embracing his methods of growth.

Growth occurs during situations that require us to stretch our faith. This means we are placed in situations that appear impossible. Trials of this kind are often overwhelming and leave us feeling hopeless. But this is when God asks us to stretch our faith and trust him despite how we feel.

Of course, we have confidence that God can deliver, but it gets difficult to believe that he will deliver when the stakes are high.

In critical situations, our faith is tested while we wait on God's response. And waiting on God to respond can make us a little uncomfortable. That's because God seems to take his time and is never really in a hurry.

We know God tests our faith in the "waiting." But thankfully, he doesn't do this merely to provoke us. Instead, he tests us for our eternal good. Besides, we would not know of his faithfulness without opportunities to trust him. Which means we only know of his deliverance to the extent our faith is tested.

Growing Despite Troubles

God desires that we become refined in holiness. And part of this process is learning more about his ways. So, we need to prioritize our relationship with him and develop a genuine trust in his provision. Once we are convinced that God is faithful and will provide all we need, we can face every hardship with confidence.

The truth tells us that we can have joy despite suffering and that we can be strong even when we are weak. But how can these things be possible?

The answer is that our close, personal relationship with God sustains us when trials seem overwhelming. Our desire to be near him and the fact that he loves us inspires perseverance. Also, knowing that God will not allow trials to defeat us inspires hope. So, we get joy simply by enduring trials because of the relationship we have with God.

It's not always easy to understand why our troubles aren't immediately removed.

Sometimes, it seems our problems stick around much longer than we would like. This is partly because we don't know the root cause of our troubles and haven't addressed core issues. At other times, God is using our trials to build resilience and strength.

In either case, God knows how to complete the work he has started. But we must know our growth is paced with exact precision. This means God has already put the necessary pieces in place to help us fulfill our destiny. We just need to keep in step with the Spirit.

Truly, we experience his precise timing every day. Sure, we might be surprised when the unexpected happens, but God is never caught off guard. In fact, he made provisions even before we were aware of our need.

God planned that Jesus would redeem mankind from the beginning. This is when the solution to our problems was set in motion. Before we had concerns, God made a way to resolve our troubles. And now, he is intimately involved in our lives executing a divine plan.

So, we can be confident knowing that God will complete what he started. We read in Heb 8:10, "I will put my laws in their minds and write them on their hearts. I will be their God, and they will be my people." Certainly, God wants us to boldly stand before him. And we can be bold because we are in Christ.

Chapter 5

Trials Are Part of God's Plan

WE FIND TRUE FULFILLMENT when we resemble Christ's nature. That means we can only be content when God is working in our lives. Sure, there are different ways to improve, but trusting God to help us through our challenges is the only path that leads to real happiness.

Trusting God means we are living by faith and learning dependance on him. Unfortunately, learning dependence is not easy. That's because most lessons on dependence are taught through our trials.

Yes, we're going to face difficulties, but every trial can be overcome by faith. Sure, certain challenges are more difficult to get through than others. And some even seem impossible to endure. But regardless of our trial's severity, each challenge is intended to teach us dependence on God.

There's a benefit to facing challenges head-on. That's because God reveals himself when we don't shy away from our trials. It's during these times when we discover who God is and that we're not alone.

We also receive blessings when we're brought closer through our trials. In other words, the hard times bring us near God so he can do a work in our hearts. That means he will use the stressful times to strengthen us and make us resilient. And even though it doesn't seem like it at the time, God uses the strain for our good.

Having Hope in the Stretching

Adversity is meant to stretch our faith and is never meant to crush or defeat us. That's because God only allows difficulties for our eternal good. Yes, he knows how to guide us toward our destiny. And if we listen carefully, we can hear him speak through our troubles. He is telling us that we can depend on his faithfulness even when our trials seem overwhelming.

When we are in the middle of our tests, it can seem easier to give up rather than allow God to stretch us. And sometimes, just having hope in his promises takes more stretching than anything else. But we must cling to what he has promised.

It may not always make sense how God is going to fulfill his promises, but we must be confident that he will. Sure, living by faith leads us into unknown places. But a lifestyle of complete trust is exactly what he wants.

God is looking for us to trust him even in our most difficult moments. If we can do that, we'll experience growth. Extraordinary displays of faith are not necessary. All God wants is simple, sincere belief.

A Promise of Better Days

God has given us his promises, but some of these promises have not yet been fulfilled. And that's okay because we know where our path ultimately leads. That's why we don't need to worry when we encounter troubles.

Better days are coming!

Revelation 21:3 says, "And I heard a loud voice from the throne saying, 'Look! God's dwelling place is now among the people, and he will dwell with them. They will be his people, and God himself will be with them and be their God.'"

God promises healing and deliverance, but until these promises are fulfilled, we must endure in faith. God doesn't want us to be afraid. Instead, we are to draw near in times of distress. But when we are afraid, his words alone bring true comfort and peace

(Matt 17:7). We can draw near to him because we know he will be our refuge and strength.

Trusting God Despite Our Difficulties

Sometimes, God's plan is different than our own, still we must offer a surrendered heart and submit to his will. Though it's difficult at times, we need to say like Jesus, "[God,] your will be done" (Matt 26:42).

We also need to be patient with God's process and not work against him. We work against him by trying to avoid discomfort. In fact, it may be God's plan that we go through tough times. This may not be something we want to hear right now, but unfortunately, it's true.

Consider Jesus who was tested by the devil (Matt 4:1) and the apostles who endured great difficulty. We are part of the same kingdom and can expect to experience similar things. We can look at these faithful examples and find encouragement knowing we don't have to face our struggles alone. It shows confidence when we say, "Let God's will be done." And when we say this, we surrender to what he decides is best for us.

We may not always understand God's plan, but faith allows us to embrace his ways. Faith also accepts that God does everything for our eternal good. And with this type of faith, we experience growth and fulfillment.

Faith Determines How We Grow

Doubts and wrong beliefs distort our understanding of God's truth. Now, we may not be intentionally led astray by these misunderstandings, but if we rely on our own knowledge we can fall away from the truth.

God wants us to be close to him so he can lead us. And if he desires to lead us, we should learn to embrace his guidance. Total trust in God does not develop quickly, rather it's formed over a lifetime. It takes a lifetime to develop because we often doubt his faithfulness.

In fact, trust develops proportionately to our faith and is based on our understanding of his faithfulness. In other words, when we believe God can do what he promised, we are able to trust that he will do it. We trust because we know God doesn't back out on commitments and we know nothing can stop him from fulfilling his promises.

However, faith is meant only for those things within his provision. Yes, miracles, prosperity, and deliverance are part of God's provision, but he is careful to do what's best in each situation. His work is extraordinary whether he simply provides strength for the journey or intervenes in some other way. But believing God only for what we want is not the way of faith. In fact, it shows a lack of trust and delays spiritual growth when we ask out of purely selfish motives.

Trusting in What God Provides

When we rely on our own understanding, we often doubt and question whether God is really acting in our best interest. It's common to question God's goodness when under the strain of adversity. Certainly, it's alarming to think we would ever say that God can't be trusted. But that's what we imply when we don't endure trials in faith.

It also shows distrust when we don't wait patiently for him to provide a way through our difficulties. We often find it difficult to wait because we want an immediate response from God to fix our problems. And when he doesn't respond quickly enough, that's when we jump into action. But that's not how growth works.

Instead, we should only want what God provides, when he chooses to provide it. This is the ultimate purpose of our trials. To teach us total dependence on God. And this includes learning to wait for his timing.

God Will Always Do What Is Best

Trust is forged over time as God reveals his faithfulness through our adversity. That means God shows us that he is near and ready to help when we face the impossible. For it is during these times that we learn he gives strength to the weak.

We can be thankful for trials because they teach us how to depend on God. Through every challenge we face, we discover that God is always there to help in our time of need. Even while we wait for deliverance, his peace keeps our hearts from losing hope.

There may come times when our hope and strength start to fade, but we can still have confidence that God will provide a way through the trouble. All we must do is embrace his process and allow him to work in our lives.

The pace at which our faith and trust grows is determined by how we respond in the refining process. So, we must not allow doubt to hinder our growth or determine how long it takes us to get through challenges. Because instead of questioning God, we need to trust and depend on him to always do what's best. And by relying on him, our relationship begins to flourish, and we become strengthened.

Content with All He Provides

Living by faith means we seek only the things that God gives. In other words, if God doesn't give it, then we don't want it. And we learn to stop acting in self-will to get what he hasn't provided.

Self-will is simply acting without God. Not only is it acting without him, but in some cases, it means acting against him. Taking this journey without God is not really an option because life separated from him only leads to sorrow.

Distress occurs when we do not surrender control to God. In other words, we experience distress when we choose self-reliance over embracing his sovereign rule in our lives. When we are self-reliant, we become reluctant to trust God. We start believing that he is not enough to meet our needs or that something else is needed beyond what he provides. This was the temptation in the garden of Eden, that life had more to offer than what God provided.

We are presented with a similar choice today. So, now we must ask ourselves, "Is God enough, or do we need something else?"

Trusting God is believing that he will provide all we need. And this kind of faith leads to a fulfilling life. Over time, we learn contentment especially as our desires are shaped by his will. Although we recognize the importance of temporary needs, our desires continue to grow for spiritual blessings.

Sometimes, we think other things bring happiness, but having God in our lives brings ultimate joy. By fully embracing his sovereignty, we learn to be satisfied with his provision. Psalm 71:5 says, "For you have been my hope, Sovereign LORD, my confidence."

Staying Focused to Have Positive Emotions

Faith and trust develop when our minds become focused on eternal principles. It's this focus that determines how we feel in difficult situations and whether we overcome our challenges with confidence.

The truth is, embracing God's eternal ways has a positive effect on our emotions. This is because our beliefs directly affect the way we feel. So, we must be careful to align our beliefs with God's truths. Surely, emotions are influenced by the thoughts we entertain. And if our thoughts are full of faith, we will experience joy. But, if we are filled with doubt, there will be unhappiness.

The way to change how we feel is through a path of surrender. Surrender requires us to relinquish control of our lives by trusting God completely. This means we are to focus all our attention on him through genuine devotion. When we draw close and give him our full attention, our happiness increases. And sometimes, shifting our focus toward God is the only thing we need to do to get more joy.

Emotions will not change until our thoughts change. In other words, the way we feel depends on whether our thoughts are being influenced by the truth. When our thoughts focus on God's promises, we feel encouraged. But, when we try to make sense of everything, doubt enters our minds. That's because growth can't occur if we rely on our knowledge alone.

However, growth happens when we focus on God's truths. And when our thoughts are focused on him, he increases our understanding to help us find meaning and purpose in difficult experiences.

True Surrender to God's Process

Faith cannot be strengthened if we keep trying to escape God's refining process. Certainly, no one wants to be in uncomfortable situations. However, living completely surrendered allows the refining process to run its full course. By abandoning self-reliance, we make a big step toward experiencing more joy and happiness.

Yes, total surrender can be a little frightening. But greater dependence doesn't always mean the loss of comfort or the absence of security. So, instead of worrying about what we give up, we must focus on who we gain. Think of total surrender more like an opportunity to grow closer to the one we love.

Many times, we get distracted by what needs to be sacrificed. But it's not about what we give up or what it costs. It's about who we gain as a beloved Lord and friend.

If we can passionately follow God in love, nothing will be too difficult to face. Our role is to remain surrendered to his process. Then he will preserve our strength when we face challenging times.

Truly, the purging process would be too difficult without a relationship that's based on love. But because of this love, we draw comfort from his presence and find encouragement in his truths. And knowing we are cherished by God helps us embrace the purging process even in our weakest moments.

Trusting God to Work in Our Lives

We can be confident that God will help us get through the tough times. Sure, we can expect deliverance but, when we don't see it, he tells us to wait in peace until our troubles pass. And we find peace by focusing on his promises and trusting in his faithfulness. However, if we focus only on our troubles it leads to doubt. But choosing to think about God's faithfulness will strengthen our confidence and fill our hearts with hope.

God's presence and mighty works should be a normal occurrence in our lives. But at times, hardships overshadow the beauty of our relationship with him. Still, he wants to have a prominent place in our lives and be able to do great things for us. However, God's works are often based on the condition that we must first become weak. That means we must become dependent on him to guide us through life's troubles.

Once we surrender, God can work in our situation. Even though we may have many abilities, our dependence on these demonstrates a lack of trust. Therefore, to trust him means that we fully rely on him for all things.

The Meaning of Strength

Self-reliance interrupts the refining process because we assert our desires above God's will. Sometimes, we do this to protect our weaknesses or to escape the pressures of his purging.

Surprisingly, it's considered an act of self-will when we guard our weaknesses. This happens when we don't allow God to fully test our limits, or when we don't open the sensitive places of our hearts.

It's self-will because our trust isn't in him to bring healing and strength. When we trust God, we abandon self-reliant behavior and start depending on him for everything we need to live a fulfilled life.

When we guard the weaknesses in our lives, we often hinder God from doing his best work. The fact is, God wants us to completely let our guard down with him. Once we completely let go, his strength will be seen in a whole new way.

God is calling us to a place of surrender. A place where the walls that separate us from his heart are removed. A place where our weaknesses are no longer hidden from his presence. The invitation has been sent. Now, the question is, will we accept his call?

By His Grace

Our lives are precious to God. However, those of us who struggle may not feel so valuable all the time. Sometimes, difficulties make us feel like we are not important or that he is ignoring our needs. Although we know this isn't true, we still feel weakened and devalued by our distress. The good news is God will help us find contentment no matter what circumstances we face. This means we'll be at peace knowing he upholds us and will not let our trials overtake us.

So, what does it really mean to have God's strength in our lives? Does it mean that all suffering will completely go away, never to return?

For some, that's exactly what it means.

However, for many, living in God's strength is the ability to endure troubles and still have joy.

When we surrender to God and allow the Spirit to work in our lives there can be true fulfillment. We find this encouragement in 2 Cor 12:9, "But he said to me, 'My grace is sufficient for you, for my power is made perfect in weakness.' Therefore I will boast all the more gladly about my weaknesses, so that Christ's power may rest on me."

Finding Strength in God's Power

When we embrace the refining process, God's power becomes evident in the way we live. In other words, his divine strength can be seen in how our hearts change and how our character grows.

Ephesians 4:24 says, "Put on the new self, created to be like God in true righteousness and holiness." This tells us that we were created, in Christ, to reflect God's nature. Not only do we reflect God's nature, but he also fills our hearts. And because God lives in us, we can trust him to guide us through every trouble.

Sometimes, it seems like God takes a long time to deliver us from our troubles. But the good news is we can endure through Christ. We read in Phil 4:13, "I can do all this through him who gives me strength."

Our situation may seem impossible, but God says anything can be done when we believe. Matthew 19:26 says, "With God all things are possible." Even when we think change and deliverance is taking too long, just know God holds time in his hands. And if we continue to believe, God ensures we will fulfill our destiny.

Who Is Faith For?

Living in faith benefits us more than it does God. That's because faith helps our limited understanding grasp eternal concepts. Faith helps us trust those things that are beyond our ability to see or comprehend. In other words, faith helps us trust God's strength even when our situation seems impossible. And faith gives us hope when our strength is gone.

Having faith helps us obtain what God has provided. For faith helps us stay strong when we feel weak and helps us overcome when things seem overwhelming.

God will make a way when we face adversity. So, it's time for us to believe we can become stronger through his power. We do not have to accept the way things have been in the past. With God working in our lives, we can expect change and growth.

Bringing Us Close in Faith

God wants to bring us near and make us like Christ through his refining process. However, this process can only be completed as we surrender. Surrendering our will and abandoning self-reliance strengthens our relationship with God. But he doesn't bring us close because of our good deeds. Instead, we are brought closer because we embrace his truths in faith. Hebrews 11:6 tells us that "without faith it is impossible to please God, because anyone who comes to him must believe that he exists and that he rewards those who earnestly seek him."

It's not enough to simply endure hardships without giving up; we must also be confident in our ability to do what God asks. It's not that we should trust in our own abilities, but we should know that God will be faithful to help us execute his plan despite hardships.

God wants us to have a courageous and an overcoming attitude. And he wants us to confront every problem knowing that he will be faithful. For we know he will never leave us to face challenges on our own, and this gives us strength and boldness.

Still, sometimes, life doesn't make sense and we end up getting disappointed. We may feel like things haven't worked out or that God has somehow let us down. We even pray but it seems like no one is there to answer. So, how can we make sense of all of this, especially when we feel like God should help us solve our problems?

Any response to such questions would not cure the aching of a broken heart. That's because a broken heart can only be comforted by the Spirit of God.

Comfort comes when we have peace with God. And when we have this peace, it gives us confidence in his faithfulness. Even though we may feel forsaken, if we draw close to him, we will be encouraged and strengthened because we'll discover that he hasn't left our side.

Our difficulties may never make sense to us, but we must remember God has an eternal perspective and he alone knows the way to a fulfilled life.

Chapter 6

Do We Trust God?

EVER WONDER WHY IT's so hard to trust God? Some of our inability to trust traces back to early experiences. These early experiences often influence whether we tend to easily trust or default to distrust. Distrust develops when we believe our emotional or physical needs will not be met or when we feel insecure or unsafe in our surroundings.

But even if these weren't everyone's early experiences, we can all develop distrust toward God anytime we feel like our needs are not being met or like we're being pushed out of our comfort zones. And, as can be expected, being distrustful of God weakens our relationship.

He Can Always Be Trusted

We all experience situations that challenge our faith. But these situations are never meant to defeat us, but to help us grow stronger. No matter what we face, God intends eternal blessings to come from our circumstances. However, if we don't believe his intentions toward us are good, we will doubt his love and doubt that he will meet our needs.

Certainly, God is not neglectful of our needs and can always be trusted. So, we must recognize that he will provide everything we need. We must also understand that nothing we go through will ever bring us eternal harm. And even though trials make it difficult to trust at times, we should never stop believing in his goodness.

Developing a strong confidence in God takes time. The reason it takes a long time is because we must correct the wrong beliefs that lead to distrust. And when we stay in God's refining process, he provides the opportunities we need to build that strong trust.

These opportunities come when our faith is challenged. That means adversity creates unique opportunities for growth. For it's in the middle of our trials where we start to develop a steady confidence.

Our confidence becomes stronger when we see God work through our circumstances. And our trust grows secure when we recognize that he is close even when we cannot sense him. Though we have our doubts, God wants to show us that we are never alone in our struggles.

Assured of His Love

Sure, it's difficult to trust God when we feel weak and vulnerable. But our confidence in God must not depend on how we feel. Instead, our confidence should be motivated by love.

However, there are times when our love for him is not enough. What we need in these moments is the assurance that God loves us. That means we can more easily trust when there is assurance of his compassion and goodness.

So, if we believe he cherishes our life, then we know he won't do anything to cause us eternal harm. These truths bring certainty and peace. When we are convinced of God's goodness, we can embrace his promises with all our hearts. And that alone is enough to bring comfort.

Doubt and Distrust at the Heart of the Issue

Doubt and distrust seem to cause more problems than any other issue a believer may face. That's because doubt erodes the very foundation of our relationship with God. It not only pulls us away from God, but in extreme cases it can also turn us against him.

So, the question we must ask is, "How can we live in faith if our minds are filled with distrust and unbelief?"

Embracing God's truths, especially when we don't feel like it, is the way we overcome unbelief. Accepting his truths is a personal decision that takes deliberate action. We might think that acting in faith comes automatically, but it doesn't. But once we learn to trust God, our faith becomes stronger and more steady.

A Mindset of Doubt

And just like acting in faith is a choice, turning away in doubt is a choice as well. So, by our choices we are either in faith or in doubt.

We must decide whether to act in faith or in doubt when facing hardships. But if we doubt too often, unbelief can become automatic and habitual. This mindset of habitual doubt can be subtle and affect even the sincerest of followers.

To test whether we have fallen into the subtle habit of doubt, simply ask, "Is there anything in my life that I am worried about?"

Jesus tells us to trust in God and not to worry (Matt 6:34).

It doesn't mean we are less of a believer for worrying, it just means there is an element of doubt that things won't work out the way we expect. Even though things don't always go as expected, what really matters is that everything works out according to God's plan. The good news is that if we stay in God's process, he will ensure that his work is finished despite our doubts.

How Do We Respond to Challenges?

It can be determined whether we are living in faith by the way we respond to challenging situations. Are we courageous? Is our trust unshakeable? Do we get discouraged?

Often, it's our unbelief that misleads us and dismisses God's faithfulness. But in challenging times, we must learn to embrace God's truths so we can overcome these negative ways of thinking.

Even though it's in our nature to question everything, we must put doubts aside and place our confidence in God. After all, he has proven to be faithful, and our doubts only weaken our relationship.

Negative Thoughts of Distrust

Old ways of thinking create conflict and tension in our relationship with God. The old self is filled with doubt, distrust, and fear. But the spiritually minded self is characterized by faith, trust, and courage.

However, we don't need to have obvious weaknesses to experience the conflict between the old self and the spiritual self. This battle exists for every believer. Not only do we all share in the same battles, but we all share in the same path to victory and joy.

This common path is our journey through God's refining process. In other words, we overcome and experience more joy in our lives as our faith is tested and we learn dependance on God.

But unbelief causes us to shrink back in disobedience. In fact, resistance to follow God's plan occurs because we lack faith and don't trust him. We may think our error is in refusing to carry out God's requests, but a closer look reveals a much bigger problem of distrust.

When our confidence in God wavers, we become reluctant to do his will. Sometimes, we hesitate to follow God's plan out of fear that his provision won't be enough or that he won't be available to help when we need him most. These negative thoughts simply overwhelm us and make it difficult to surrender.

So, when our minds are filled with discouragement and doubt, we miss the blessing that comes from relying on God's promises.

Live by Faith and Find Strength

God wants us dependent on his strength so our lives can resemble Christ's. Just like he did for Jesus, God will supply the Spirit when we willingly offer our faith and obedience. But when we have shortcomings, it's because we have not relied on God's power but on our own abilities.

Even though it may not be possible to reach perfection in this life, we must strive to be obedient to God in all things. So, we might question, "Won't God ask me to do something difficult if I try to obey everything he says?"

The answer is "yes," but we are comforted knowing God doesn't ask us to do something he will not give us the grace to accomplish.

Just because we are doing what God asked doesn't mean everything will be easy or that our circumstances will change instantly. Sometimes, we can have trust in God and not see any positive results at all. Or at least not from what we can tell.

But, we must remember, we are in a growing season, and it's hard to see things as they grow. For growth is most noticeable only at specific stages of development. So, if we're not seeing any changes, don't be discouraged, we just haven't reached the stage where growth is visible. We are still a work in progress and at the right time we are going to see a difference.

God's strength is revealed in our weakness, and it's in his refining process where we learn to surrender self-will and become empowered by the Spirit. As we grow less reliant on self, God becomes more prominent in our lives. And when God becomes the focus of our affection, we will be strengthened to overcome challenges.

We learn as we grow in God's strength that trials serve a significant role. For he uses challenges to remove self-reliance from our lives and to reveal his strength in us. If we are not seeing his power in our lives, it's because there is still self-will to surrender.

We increase God's strength in our lives by becoming more dependent on him, especially in the small decisions we make. Asking him how he would like us to approach everyday situations helps us learn submission to his will.

However, trying to remove self-will through our own efforts doesn't replace God's refining process. In fact, there is no substitute to the lessons we learn through adversity.

God's Side Is the Winning Side

When troubles knock us down, we sometimes think God doesn't care about our suffering. These moments make it hard to focus on him, but if we are convinced of his goodness, we can endure anything. So, if we are to endure our trials in faith, we must have a clear understanding of his nature.

We see a good example of how God's people struggled with doubt in Num 14:6–9. And just like the children of Israel, who forgot that God was on their side and wouldn't allow them to fail, we also forget when we're faced with difficulties. But the danger in forgetting about God's nature is that it leads to doubt and causes us to question his plan for our lives.

So, instead of doubting like the children of Israel, let us be more like Joshua and Caleb, who looked to God's strength rather than the enemy's ability. For they declared in faith that they could accomplish God's will regardless of the challenges that were before them. They remembered God's mighty works and knew he could be trusted.

Their faith was strengthened the more they focused on God's ability and trustworthiness. And the same is true for us today. The more we focus on God's faithfulness, the more we can depend on him to get us through our trials.

Many of our troubles would diminish if we could get a correct view of God. He is mighty, masterful, and majestic. Truly, there aren't any words that can adequately describe our God. How wonderful to know that this holy, awesome, and powerful God is fighting on our side. It's amazing!

However, there are a couple things that need to be mentioned here. Realistically, God does not need to fight because there is nothing or no one who can contend with him. Also, we need to be on his side, the winning side, to get these benefits. And since we are the children of the Living God, these truths give us confidence.

So, like Joshua and Caleb, we must think and declare by faith that God is our strength.

Having Strong Faith When We Are Weak

Even though having faith like Joshua and Caleb may take a lifetime to develop, we can start today by believing God will fulfill his promises and give victory over our challenges. That means we can have contentment and joy no matter what we're going through.

Certainly, God can turn where we are now into a promised land. The challenges we face today that seem impossible are not too difficult for him. He equips us with enough strength to overcome every situation, even if our weaknesses remain part of our lives.

We might say, "How can I be strong when I feel so weak?" Ironically, this is exactly what relying on God looks like. Sometimes, we don't feel what God says we have. In fact, we are strong only when there is dependence on God's power. Consider it a good thing when our weaknesses place us in situations where God alone can help.

Our role is to yield our will to God's strength and embrace his truths by faith. This allows God to take over and complete his work. We may not always understand what God is doing, but we still need to trust and believe.

When Feelings Don't Line Up with the Truth

Embracing God's promises based on his word alone is an act of trust. And, over time, we eventually feel the joy and contentment that accompanies our beliefs. So, this means we must choose faith over our feelings and truth over our circumstances.

It is not always easy to reconcile our feelings with the truth. This means we can experience distress even though God tells us we can have joy and happiness. And just because we know God has a greater purpose in our trials doesn't automatically remove feelings of despair.

We're often in situations where we don't feel what God says we rightfully have. He says we are strong, courageous, and able. But instead, we sometimes feel weak, anxious, and feeble. But even when our feelings don't agree with the truth, we are still asked to pursue God through faith and sincere trust.

But we don't need giant faith in these moments. It only takes simple, sincere belief that God will be with us.

Out of a trust so small comes many mighty works. Miracles happen, doors open, and prayers get answered. Great things happen when our confidence is in God. And we have confidence in God because he keeps his promises.

God always has been, and will always be, faithful. He doesn't change. He will keep his word.

Sure, living by faith will put us in uncomfortable situations. But God promised to be faithful and grant us favor when we sow faith from a dependent heart.

So, when we face difficulties, we must choose to trust God even if our circumstances appear impossible. For this is our journey to the promised land. And since this is our journey, we must believe until we reach the end.

We Live by Faith, Not by Feelings

Our thoughts can stop us from enjoying life. But if we want to have true contentment, we shouldn't focus on temporary concerns. Instead, we should view situations from an eternal perspective. For an eternal perspective helps us understand the meaning behind our difficulties.

Sure, it can be hard to see God's purpose in our troubles. And it can be difficult to see how adversity is used for our good. But understanding God has an eternal reason for our circumstances gives us hope and courage.

Since our emotions change with our circumstances, faith shouldn't be based on how we feel. It's strange how we can know something is true, but not feel it in our hearts. We may know God loves us but feel like he doesn't care about our difficulties. Or we may believe God will never cause us harm but still feel overwhelmed by our trials.

We must recognize that our feelings won't always agree with the truth. So, instead of blindly following our emotions, we must base our faith on God's truths alone.

A New Way of Thinking

For so long, in the old self, we followed whatever truths were supported by our own reason and emotions. If it felt right, it must have been right. There was no need to doubt these thoughts. But God revealed a different way of thinking. Now, in the new self, we confront our old understanding with his truths.

Sure, it can be unsettling when he challenges our way of thinking and perceiving life. But God wants to take us through a process that will purge unhelpful views from our lives. Unfortunately, this process is not quick or easy.

The Opposite of How We Feel

Achieving happiness always involves embracing truth. And life satisfaction only comes when we know and accept what God has said.

Many times, God shows us the path to peace by requesting we act opposite of our feelings. In other words, he often requires of us what hurts most during the purging process. For he asks us to believe despite our doubts, trust when we feel abandoned, and be courageous when we are afraid. God works in ways beyond our understanding, but through these methods his wisdom and power are revealed.

God says we can have what is impossible in the natural to have. That means that forgiveness can flow from a heart once filled with pain, that hope can be found in times of desperation, and that our weaknesses can be overshadowed by resilience and strength.

These truths exist only with God. That's because the impossible can happen when we embrace his process. But we must accept God's will before his works can be revealed.

So, if he is calling us to trust him, we should follow his path with all our hearts. No, it won't be easy, but if we go where he leads, his plan will be so much better than we could possibly imagine.

Adversity Is Never Meant to Defeat Us

Sometimes, it can seem like we're not growing during difficult times, especially when our weaknesses and imperfections continue to surface. But even though we might disagree with God's process, we can be confident that he has a reason behind his methods.

Not only do we need to remember these truths, but we also need to embrace the fact that God is supreme ruler over all things. And when we accept God's rule, we allow him total control of our circumstances. That means we also allow him to determine the duration and intensity that accompanies every difficulty.

Certainly, releasing control can be uncomfortable at first, but in the end, it brings peace and joy.

God's truths say we have his strength when we are weak. And this brings contentment. So, we must focus on these eternal truths and not on what our emotions tell us. But listening to our emotions and avoiding difficulties cause us to lose focus on what's most important.

We must remember, suffering is not the purpose of our trials. Our challenges are meant to strengthen our faith, develop Christ-like character, and reveal God's presence in our lives. In other words, adversity is never intended to defeat us but to build us up in Christ.

Our Response to the Test

God has a unique way of purifying the lives of his people. He uses difficulties, challenges, and adversity to refine our hearts. Sometimes, we are immersed in the trial; at other times troubles and adversity gradually build up.

No matter how these circumstances arise, they are typically not very pleasant. However, we can have confidence that God is completing his work in us. Proverbs 17:3 says, "The crucible for silver and the furnace for gold, but the LORD tests the heart."

It's difficult to endure trials without a passion for God. But if we could only find out what keeps us from embracing his rulership and learn to trust him, then we would find joy in this journey again.

When we're overburdened by our troubles, it doesn't always seem possible to have joy. But if we accept that God has a purpose for our trials, we can be comforted and encouraged. And even though we do not always understand his ways, we can know he loves us (1 John 4:9–10) and performs all things for our eternal good (Rom 8:28).

So, what should we do when we encounter adversity?

Paul and Silas show exactly what to do.

In Acts 16:25 we see them praying and singing praises to God. Paul and Silas had been whipped, feet bound in stocks, and locked away in prison. In all this, they still chose to pray and offer praise.

So now we ask, "What can be done to find joy when we are tested?"

The first thing we can do is talk to God about our experiences. For we learn dependence by opening our hearts completely to him during difficult times. And then, praise him. This is not just acknowledging him as supreme ruler of all creation. Rather, it's being thankful that he is in control of every aspect of our lives.

This means we need to have gratitude for what he's provided and acknowledge his goodness in every situation.

As a result, joy and contentment begin to develop in the middle of our challenges, especially as we open our hearts and surrender to his plan.

Chapter 7

Strengthened to Endure Challenges

SO, WHAT DO WE really want when we're facing difficulties or hardships? The truth seems obvious, but many times, we just want our situation to change. And it doesn't really matter how our situation changes. We just want things to be different than the way they are. Sometimes, we're satisfied simply believing God is about to do something different. We're satisfied because we know things won't remain the same. And certainly, if God is at work, things will get better!

But when we pray and nothing seems to change, it can feel like we're facing difficulties alone and like God has abandoned us. That's especially true when trials have become too difficult to endure. But instead of giving in to despair, we must embrace God's truths and persevere in faith.

However, trying to face our challenges without faith only leads to uncertainty and fear. But this is not how we were meant to live. In fact, living in a state of unbelief is contrary to the new self we have been given in Christ. Not only does a mindset of unbelief go against the new self, but it also leads to unhappiness.

God is with us during our troubles and wants us to be confident in his faithfulness. Unfortunately, our doubts question whether he is willing to help when we need him most. But despite these doubts, our hearts should cry to God for deliverance.

God will hear and save us, but we must know his deliverance is not always smooth and easy. That's because he works in ways that try our faith. In other words, God will not change our circumstances just so we can be comfortable or be at ease. Instead, his focus is to develop character and resilience as we go through our trials.

God is not so much concerned with making everything comfortable for us. That's because he works to develop strength and contentment within our hearts. Although we expect deliverance out of our circumstances, God often strengthens us to endure. In fact, it may not even be in our best interest to escape what is putting pressure on our lives. Many times, it is this strain that allows growth and change to occur.

Wanting everything to be easy and comfortable means we are focused on temporary concerns. Sure, it's not wrong to want relief or deliverance, but our desires begin to shift once we have an eternal focus. When we have an eternal focus, it becomes our greatest passion to do God's will, even if it means enduring discomfort.

Whether we prosper or endure discomfort, the only thing that matters is being found in the center of God's will. Yes, it's easier to follow his path when the future seems paved with good fortune. But this may not always be our experience. That's because we are often asked to embrace hardships as part of our journey.

We must recognize that happiness, joy, and satisfaction in life result from doing God's will, even if that means embracing difficulty. It's important to know that he will never ask us to go through adversity, then leave us to face it alone.

Truly, we are never alone, and we can find refuge in the center of his will. And it's in the center of his will where we fully encounter his presence.

Not Striving against the Process

God will uphold us by his strength when we face trials. Now, this doesn't mean we will be perfect in everything we do. Instead, it means our faith and trust in God will outlast any difficulty. And that no matter what happens, we will cling to him.

To experience a life of happiness and peace, we must submit and surrender to God's will. Of course, we typically don't have a problem submitting and surrendering to his will until it makes us uncomfortable. But, sometimes, when faced with pressure and strain, we become resistant to his plan.

Striving against God's purpose causes unhappiness. And remaining at odds with his plan weakens the relationship we have with him.

However, when we surrender to God's process, discontentment and unhappiness are removed. For the truth changes us in the refining process. That's because the truth confronts our false beliefs and changes the way we feel. Once we have completely embraced this process, we will begin to experience more happiness and satisfaction in life.

If we are to endure adversity with patience, we must focus on the eternal purpose of our trials. And we must be confident that God can be trusted to care for us when we're hurt and discouraged. For he promised that he would not allow our difficulties to defeat us if we continue to trust him.

Making Something Beautiful in Our Lives

We must understand that God uses trials to create something unique in us. Even though it doesn't make sense right now, he is using difficulties to beautify our lives with Christlikeness.

Christlikeness develops over time, and embracing God's process allows our character to be refined and tested. Initially, when we are tested, we may not see any growth. But eventually, Christlikeness appears out from weakness. This means something heavenly springs forth from our struggle as God helps us express Christ's nature.

Our challenges accomplish more than we know. At the start of a trial, we enter unrefined. But when the master has completed his work, we are purified and formed into a heavenly vessel.

Proverbs 25:4 says, "Remove the dross from the silver, and a silversmith can produce a vessel."

Self-will is an example of "dross."

Sometimes, we resist God's work in our lives just so we can remain comfortable. But obtaining comfort in this life should not be our only desire. Our highest priority is to honor God and be found pleasing in his sight. Therefore, we need to allow him to refine and shape us so we can be a beautiful vessel. A vessel crafted by God's will.

God considers every detail when making his masterpieces.

We may feel alone right now, but be encouraged because the master is giving us his full attention. Believe it or not, he is completely focused on our lives. When our trials have been prolonged, it is easy to think God has somehow forgotten about us. But vessels of great value take time to make and remain in the refiner's fire a little longer. Though the reasons for God's timing may not be fully understood, we know the purpose for the difficulty is to bring us blessings.

Vessels in the Refiner's Fire

The details are important when God works on his masterpieces. Some vessels of honor have more features than others, but he creates them all for his pleasure. God is not trying to impress people. In fact, he has his own standards which are far beyond anything we can imagine.

Also, he creates according to his own purpose. Certain vessels may be created with significant detail but be only for his eyes to behold. This is one reason why many of us secretly endure hardships and experience his mighty works without anyone ever knowing. It's only for his eyes!

We don't always know why God's paths lead us into adversity. For his ways are far above our own. But, thankfully, someday we will know his ways perfectly.

Some vessels are simple and some elaborate, but regardless of the vessel's complexity, God values them the same. He also knows how to complete his work. For he is making masterpieces of us all. So, if we stay in the process, God will make us complete in Christ.

Limited Thinking Won't Help Us Understand God's Plan

We should learn to identify and confront wrong thinking so we can follow God's will. We find a few examples of where wrong mindsets hindered people from seeing the will of God during the life and ministry of Jesus.

In John 11:1–44 we see that Lazarus was sick but died because Jesus's arrival was delayed. Martha said to Jesus, "Lord if you had only been here, Lazarus would not have died."

Like Martha, we often make the mistake of using our limited knowledge to understand God's master plan. We try to understand God's plan, but sometimes it can be difficult to make sense of what he's doing. Of course, there are times when everything adds up, and we understand exactly how God will use our circumstances. But it seems most things remain unknown and must be embraced by faith.

However, we must not put common understanding ahead of God's leading. This means we are to avoid using limited knowledge in situations that require an eternal perspective. This is what Martha's example teaches.

As it relates to us today, if we are guided by our old way of thinking, our focus will only be on temporary concerns. But if we allow God to guide us, our thoughts will be focused on eternal matters.

Martha eventually recognized that Jesus was able to manage her situation and meet her needs. Likewise, we must have the same faith that says, "Jesus, even though my situation looks impossible, I know you can handle what I'm going through!"

We can rest and be confident knowing whatever we're facing is not too difficult for God.

We must be able to accept that God is not always going to remove every obstacle. However, he will always help us overcome. Not only does God help us get through difficulties, but he also gives us joy and peace in the process. And like Martha did, we are to recognize God's sovereignty over our circumstances. And by doing this, our troubles will fade into the background.

Our trust in God is never wasted because he always comes through for his children. And just like Jesus did for Lazarus, he will bring life into our situation. That means we will have the comfort, strength, and encouragement we need to overcome.

Rigid Views Stop Us from Seeing God

We also must avoid overlooking truth because we have become too rigid in our views.

We see in Mark 14:1 that the chief priests and scribes plotted against Jesus. The chief priests and scribes were entrusted to be the spiritual leaders of Israel, yet here they are seeking the death of God's only Son.

God is often dismissed when we get stuck thinking that things must be done our way. However, we must embrace truth wherever it leads. Learning to hold our beliefs with openness allows opportunities for God to reveal himself. The priests and scribes assumed they had complete knowledge of God and yet they could not recognize the works he performed right in front of them.

We should not hold on to anything that God could not take freely from us. If there's a belief that we won't allow him to change then we haven't truly surrendered. We need to surrender not only wrong beliefs about God, but wrong beliefs about ourselves as well. To experience change, God needs to be approached with a submitted heart. And when our heart is humble, the truth can easily guide us.

Our views must be grounded in the truth so that we're not led away from God. Even though we might have good reasons for our views, we must recognize that our understanding is limited.

The chief priests and scribes neglected to see the truth in the law and were blinded by self-righteousness and pride. If we're not careful, we can also be blinded by these same biases. And today, if we are too rigid in our thinking, we will not be able to perceive God's path. In other words, if we do not bend to God's ways, we won't be able to learn or understand his truths.

Knowing God Means We Know His Love

Having an awareness of God's compassion puts our troubles in perspective. Often, we get too focused on our own problems and lose sight of God's love. This is what happened in Mark 4:38 when the disciples thought they would perish in a storm out at sea. The disciples asked why Jesus didn't do anything to help and wondered if he cared about them at all.

Don't we feel the same way sometimes?

Uncertain if God cares.

This is especially true when our troubles are overwhelming and things don't seem to change. So, when the storms of life get out of control, remember that God is paying close attention. And that he loves us and would never let anything cause us eternal harm. We know this because Jesus eventually calmed the storm, showing the disciples he cared despite their fears.

The same is true for us today; God cares about our situation and will calm our troubles. So, if we are assured of God's love, then our confidence in him will grow during trials regardless of how things appear.

Certainly, a lack of faith causes us to lose hope. But trusting God helps us overcome these feelings of despair. We know trust is forged over time, but as trust is being formed, our love for God keeps us encouraged. However, the love we have for God is really a response to his compassion for us. And knowing he cares assures us of his goodwill.

Also, to know him is to know of his affection. For God desires to be with us and is passionate about his relationship with his people. Exodus 34:14 says, "Do not worship any other god, for the LORD, whose name is Jealous, is a jealous God." God cares for his people. But to misunderstand his love is to not really know him.

Our Feelings Can Mislead Us

In Luke 10:30–37, Jesus talks about a Samaritan's compassion upon a certain man who was robbed and wounded. Jesus said this man was passed over by a priest, then later by a Levite, but finally the Samaritan stopped to offer aide.

In this story, we understand how values and personal bias influenced decisions about helping someone in need. And it's safe to assume that emotions were also a factor in helping guide some of these decisions.

Compassion led the Samaritan to help, and repulsion caused the priest and Levite to avoid. In each case, emotions influenced how they were thinking and how they interpreted their own values.

So, as it pertains to us today, we should not allow our emotions alone to determine our values. For we should be led by truth and not by our feelings. That's because emotions can cloud our thinking and skew the truth. In fact, God's truths are often manipulated because of emotions. No doubt, our emotions serve a role, but God's truths are to be the standard for our values and the Spirit is to be the guide for our thinking.

Hope for the Journey

We were never promised an easy journey, just one that leads to an abundant life. To have an abundant life means we must let go of the things that interrupt the Spirit's work. Yes, God knows we need comfort. But if we commit to God's process when it's tough, he will comfort us until we sense the strength that comes from believing his truths.

Sometimes, trials can be so difficult that they shake even the strongest faith. That's when we are tempted to doubt God's truths altogether. What we may not realize is that problems often get worse when we lose hope.

However, when we are firmly convinced of God's faithfulness, thoughts of doubt and despair fade. But trusting in God's goodness doesn't mean our experiences will always be pleasant.

Certainly, trusting God can lead us into hardships and difficulties. But adversity helps us face life with confidence. And even though we face trials, knowing God is orchestrating our lives gives us the hope we need to make it through.

Chapter 8

God's Faithfulness Revealed

FAITH IS ESSENTIAL IF we really want to know God. That's because unbelief causes confusion. It confuses our perception of God's truths and corrupts our understanding of his nature. In other words, unbelief causes us to think God is unloving when we are tested. What's interesting is unbelief produces more doubtful thinking if it's not confronted with the truth and leads to a weakened relationship with God.

But we know a doubtful mindset isn't right and will not help us overcome. For without faith, we can't have hope or peace. So, even though we experience distress, the right mindset is to keep our faith firmly in God.

Focusing on God's truths keeps us encouraged and balanced. We also feel better about life and experience more happiness when our minds are filled with the truth. It's certain, what we focus on will consume our thoughts. So, by focusing on God's truths, our thoughts will overflow with faith and hope. And this overflow leads to an eternal perspective and an abundant life.

Remember What God Has Done

If we think about it, God has helped us overcome every challenge. And he has shown us that we can count on him when we face our troubles. When we look back at everything we have been through, we can see that he has always been with us. Even now he is with us and wants us to find rest in him. But our emotions can make it difficult to stay in his rest, especially when our feelings conflict with what we know to be true.

So, it's important for us to remember that just because our feelings change doesn't mean his truths change. That means we can always have peace and fulfillment. Thankfully, this peace is not something we need to earn. For it has been freely given in Christ (Heb 4:1–11). And that truth will never change.

Truth Is Understood with the Spiritual Mind

Sometimes, we think God's promises will never come to pass. But these thoughts happen because we have unbelief. Thankfully, God doesn't depend on our unwavering faith to fulfill his promises. Instead, he made promises based on his own faithfulness.

We never have to worry whether he is going to keep his side of the deal. In fact, God's plan is going to happen just like he said it would. And the promises we cling to will happen simply because he is faithful.

Even though we know these truths, we can still get discouraged when our feelings don't support what we believe. Sadly, the difference between what we believe and how we feel is a reality that's all too common. That's because God's principles are understood with the spiritual mind and our emotions are influenced by the old self. We see this in Scripture.

Matthew 5:44 asks us to love our enemies. But even though we embrace the truth that God wants us to show love, we may still feel hurt or bitterness against a person because of some offence. So, here we can believe one thing, but feel something else entirely different. God uses these differences in our emotions as opportunities to bring change into our lives. Therefore, change and growth occur when we embrace God's truths despite how we feel.

Benefiting from Trials

However, just going through a trial doesn't guarantee we'll benefit from that experience. In fact, the opposite can be true. If there's doubt and distrust, we can become bitter because of misunderstandings about hardships. But if difficulties are endured faithfully, we'll come out of the experience knowing more about God.

To benefit from adversity, we must have the right perspective. That means we must become convinced that God will not allow us to suffer eternal harm. Surely, he protects us from harm and gives us strength when we are weak. With the right perspective, we can have confidence that all things will be used for our good.

Grateful for Our Bond with God

It's difficult having hope in God's promises when our minds are filled with doubt. But instead of doubting, he wants us to be assured of his goodness. Not only can we know of his goodness, but he also wants us to experience his kindness. And we can see his kindness when our hearts become grateful for what he provides.

But many times, we take for granted what God has provided. Truly, our hearts would be grateful if we could only see his hand orchestrating the ordinary and supplying the simple. It's this gratefulness that leads to happiness and fulfillment.

Yes, we can be happy even in the middle of our difficulties. Just knowing that he wants to give us good things can bring joy into our lives. That's because no matter the challenge, we know he is with us. Gratefulness fills our hearts because we know God has given us everything even though he doesn't owe us anything.

Because God freely gave his only son, we now have eternal life. God was not required to send Jesus but was obligated by his own promise to provide a way of salvation. And now, having accepted God's way of redemption, we must seek to preserve our bond with him. Jude 1:21 says, "Keep yourselves in God's love as you wait for the mercy of our Lord Jesus Christ to bring you to eternal life."

Trials try to erode our devotion to God and strain the bond we have with him. This is due to the nature of challenges. For adversity strikes at the heart of our weaknesses and seeks to remove our faith in God.

But thankfully there's hope.

For strength comes out of weakness because God brings to life what is sown in faith. And even if our strength fails, we will be upheld by God's power. He loves us, and places significant value on our lives. This means he will not allow us to be defeated by our troubles. And knowing how valuable and important we are to him gives us hope, which helps us endure.

Experiencing God's Strength in Our Weakness

How we view our relationship with God determines our happiness. That's because knowing our value to him can bring encouragement and strength. But we need to be convinced that his love toward us is unending.

The problem is we often question God's love and his intentions when times get tough. Even though we know God is devoted to us, we can't help but ask, "Why does he allow hardships?"

This is a sincere question, but distance is created in our relationship when we doubt his goodness. This distance erodes the very foundation of our Christian experience. It causes us to deny his love and makes our affection for him dependent on comfort.

We must remember that God uses trials for our eternal benefit. This may not make things any easier right now, but at least we can be encouraged knowing he has a divine purpose for our trials. Strength can emerge from adversity. And this is true even when our circumstances don't change.

Right now, our situation may look impossible, but we have hope, and hope is all we need sometimes to get through. Just knowing God is in control and has not forgotten us can be comforting enough.

No matter what it feels like, we have God's complete attention. There's no situation too big or too small for him to handle.

For God views every concern as important. We know God counts the hairs on our head, and this tells us that he is attentive to every detail of our life.

Enriched by What God Provides

God wants us to experience his goodness right now. And although our current circumstances may not be pleasant, we'll have more joy and fulfillment once we consider the eternal significance of our situation. By shifting our views to an eternal perspective, we start to see how God guides us to fulfill our purpose.

But to get an eternal perspective we must find God's will in the trial. Sure, it's helpful to know whether we should expect circumstances to change or if we must overcome them in faith. However, God's plans are not always revealed ahead of time. So, when our path is unclear, we should not try to guess at what God is doing but should simply yield to his plan as it unfolds.

Adversity enriches our relationship with God and provides opportunities to experience his love. But a wrong understanding of the truth causes problems in our connection with him. Sometimes, we can misinterpret God's promises and begin to think we are entitled to a life free from adversity. And at the sight of trouble, we try to use his promises to acquire comfort.

But we must remember that God is not obligated to meet our demands on our terms. We make the mistake of acting as if he should serve our own interests. Although he meets our needs, his promises serve an eternal purpose. And when we place our desires above God's purpose it causes separation, but humility will bring us close and prepare us for his blessings. So, instead of using his promises just to find comfort, we need to seek out his promises to find his purpose.

Seeing God in Our Trials

Jesus said the pure in heart are "blessed" because they will see God (Matt 5:8). When we rely on God, we start to notice his work in everyday situations. Learning dependence on God teaches us to see the difference between what we do through our own efforts and what he is doing in our lives.

The pure in heart also see God in the middle of their trials. This means we recognize that he is the same whether we experience blessings or difficulty. Certainly, confidence flows naturally when life is easy, but spiritual growth occurs during the tough times. For it is during the tough times when our faith needs to be firmly placed in God.

Faith and trust must guide us through adversity because our emotions are often unstable and unreliable. That means our focus needs to be on God instead of our problems. When God becomes our highest priority, troubles begin to fade. And no matter what we face, we can endure if our full attention is on him.

A Day of Deliverance

At any moment, we can experience divine deliverance from our troubles. Sometimes, God will directly intervene and instantly change our circumstances. At other times, he strengthens us for adversity.

No matter the situation, we can be assured that God's deliverance will eventually come. Believers, who endure faithfully, will ultimately see God in the end. Our minds can't really imagine what that day will be like. But we too often lose sight of what is awaiting us in the future. So, instead of looking at our challenges, we should learn to refocus our thoughts on what's up ahead at Christ's promised appearing.

We have been promised that better days are coming. It's encouraging to know that our current experiences are not what we were promised. God said there is coming a day when pain, death, and crying will cease (Rev 21:4). It's this hope that gives us comfort and confidence in difficult times. Like Job, we need to focus on what awaits us (Job 25–26). Right now, we wait for Christ to be revealed. And when he finally comes back, our trials will end, and our sorrows will be no more (1 John 3:2).

Joy Awaits Us in the Future

The sufferings we experience are temporary. For our sorrows will eventually be erased by heavenly joy. And when that day comes, happiness will go on forever. And because we know all pain will come to an end, we can be content. Just believing that God will fulfill these promises gives us hope and confidence.

Suffering is not part of our eternal future. The adversity we face is only a small part of a much larger plan. In the Scripture, we are compared to athletes who endure adversity so they can win and obtain a much greater reward. Athletes believe their achievements are worth the demands of training and pressures of competition. Our hardships could be perceived in a similar way. We are to be focused on the prize awaiting us in the future. This hope helps us endure challenges and disappointments. No matter our current experiences, it should be considered a small price compared to the eternal reward that is in Christ (Phil 3:14).

He Carries Us When We Are Weak

When we understand God's ways, we know how to accept both blessings and adversity with a grateful heart. God didn't promise an easy path, but he did say we would have his favor. And knowing this truth helps us embrace hardships. For fulfillment comes when we face our challenges in God's strength. But if we run from adversity, it will only rob us of true comfort.

God carries us when it seems impossible to make it through our circumstances. We may feel faint right now, but, somehow, we are able to continue our journey. It's not necessarily our tenacity that keeps us going; rather, God upholds us during these times.

Sure, we would like him to infuse us with might and strength, but this is not always his chosen path. That's because, sometimes, he reveals his strength by sustaining us when we are weak.

Doing Great Things Despite Our Limitations

Surprisingly, our weaknesses serve a role in God's plan. We might wonder how weakness could ever be part of anything God does. But our weaknesses serve a significant role. This is because in our frailty, God's power becomes our strength. And when we need help, he shows up to deliver.

Our weaknesses and limitations do not prevent us from accomplishing God's work. That's because he can do great things despite our inadequacies. We don't need to be perfect for him to work in our lives. Instead, he desires to work with surrendered hearts.

Now, it's true that our lives are usually marked by something we believe to be unsuitable for the master. But regardless of these feelings, our love for God should help us move beyond these fears. And since we know God loves us, we can be confident that he will provide the strength we need to fulfill his plan.

Our trust in God gets stronger the more we understand that he wants to do good things for us. Also, knowing he is good and uses trials to bring eternal blessings teaches us not to be discouraged when facing difficulties (Rom 8:35–39). And although our trials may not seem good right now, if they are given to God, he will use them to make an eternal difference.

Nothing escapes God's attention when bringing these eternal blessings to his children. Regardless of how difficult our situation has become, know that we haven't been overlooked or forgotten. Even though we might be facing trials right now, we can be assured that God's purpose for our life involves divine blessings. This gives us confidence that he is orchestrating his plan even now. So, we must continue to hope in his promises and trust his faithfulness.

Chapter 9

God's Promises Are True

THE WAY WE APPROACH life determines how we feel. If we are confident in God's promises, we will feel encouraged. But doubting his compassion causes us to feel abandoned and alone. And these doubts cause us to question whether he will help when we need him most.

Even though it may not seem true right now, God is committed to helping us in difficult times. He loves us more than we can imagine and has promised to be with us when things get tough. But unfortunately, we don't always believe this to be true.

Certainly, many of our doubts come from misunderstanding God's love. But the Scriptures clearly say he cares about us (John 3:16). And since the Scriptures say so, it makes it hard to deny the reality of his affection.

Being Influenced by the Truth

When emotions influence our beliefs, our faith in God becomes unstable. That's because emotions can confuse the truth. But our faith shouldn't be based on the way we feel. Instead, our faith should be grounded in the truth.

As we already know, feelings do not provide an objective standard for the truth. That's because when we base our beliefs on feelings, it distorts truths about God. It also distorts truths about his love and our ability to cope with adversity.

But we must get to the place where we can look beyond our feelings to see the truth. This means when we don't feel God's love, we still know his compassion never changes. And when we can't see how to cope, we still know we can endure all things through his strength.

Sometimes, we make the mistake of trusting our feelings instead of God's truths. During tough times it's easy to think we can't make it. However, the truth says, he will help us handle stress and disappointment. We often take God out of the equation when trying to solve our problems. But there is good news: he is here, right now, and will be with us when troubles arise again. There is no need to worry. God has committed himself to us and he always keeps his promises.

Resolving Difficult Questions

We might ask, "If God is concerned about us, then why does he often remain silent when we need him?" Or "Why does he allow us to feel overwhelmed at times?"

These are questions each of us must resolve if we are to find fulfillment. We must be able to accept that God is both silent and attentive. And that he permits difficulty to teach greater dependence. Even though God is silent at times, he is still fully devoted to us and will provide everything we need to find fulfillment. So, if we must endure hardships, it is for our good.

We must trust God during the silent seasons and recognize that he uses difficult times to draw us near and bring new growth. In fact, we grow strong only when our faith is tested. Sure, trials will still be tough, but we will be happy because we are growing. But if we want to continue growing, we must embrace God's path through adversity. For happiness is found only when we follow his way.

Drawn to Jesus Because of His Love

The story in Matt 9:19–22 shows us how God is concerned about our suffering and proves he is not too busy for our problems. We see in the Scripture that Jesus was on his way to raise a certain man's daughter from the dead. No doubt, this was a very urgent matter for Jesus and a miracle that would attest to his very own resurrection. So, we can picture the importance of Jesus going on this journey. However, as he was leaving, a woman who needed healing thought she would just touch the hem of his garment. This woman believed by doing this she would be healed.

So why did she only touch the hem of Jesus's garment and not ask for his full attention?

Maybe it was too crowded, maybe she was too embarrassed, or maybe she was simply content with just touching the hem of his garment.

While we can only speculate, we must answer for ourselves, "Why are we okay with avoiding Jesus's full attention?" In other words, why don't we fully expose our hearts to him? Could it be that we think our needs aren't important or that we believe God doesn't care about our troubles?

While we may not view God as cruel or unkind, we sometimes question our value and worth to him. But questioning his love for us erodes our faith in him. And when we believe his love for us is insincere, we stop drawing close to him.

Sometimes, we believe adversity stays around because we don't deserve change. Often, these beliefs come from a sense of low self-worth. These beliefs cause us to think that our problems are too insignificant for God. And it seems our hardships only reinforce these beliefs.

However, thinking that we are not important to God doesn't agree with what we know is true. We know he cares and pays attention to our problems. But, sometimes, it still seems like he is "looking" the other way.

It can feel like God has forgotten about us, especially when we are facing difficulties and others are being blessed. We see God providing ease for others and we ask, "What about me?"

It's tempting to think God is not concerned about our needs or is too busy to help us. Even though these thoughts do not align with the truth, we still feel like we are not worthy of our miracle. But our hearts must reach for Jesus in faith even when we do not feel valued. Because if we don't see our true importance to God, we'll never draw near in times of distress.

We can become so absorbed in trying to solve temporary problems, we forget God has a much bigger plan. God honors faith and will answer prayer, but only as it promotes our eternal good. Sometimes, answering prayers our way may not be what we really need. Because what we really need, ultimately, is God's comfort. Not for his sake, but for our own.

God doesn't want us to feel overwhelmed by our challenges. That's because being overburdened leads to desperation and causes us to seek our own solutions. But we are to reach out to Jesus like the woman in Matt 9. And even if we must draw close with insecurities and touch the "hem of his garment," that will be enough to bring peace.

We notice, in Matt 9:22, that Jesus stopped what he was doing and spoke to this woman. He turned his attention to her and said that her faith had made her whole. This tells us that we should keep trusting and believing despite unfavorable circumstances. And as we continue to seek God in faith, he will reward us with his presence.

Faithful to Give Eternal Life

How we experience God's presence is not always predictable. Sometimes, we have a very real sense of his presence, near and intimate. At other times, he seems distant and silent. But regardless of how we feel, we learn about his commitment to us through Scripture. And the truth helps us remain confident that he is near regardless of how we feel. This helps us trust that he is close in our trials.

God's faithfulness is shown in his promise to give eternal life to all who believe. This new life in our hearts is not merely a higher moral standard, but God's very presence (Rom 8:11). And embracing this new life is the only way to true happiness. That's because it means we have been emptied of self and filled with the Spirit. And just like Jesus, we must abandon self-reliance and become completely dependent on God. This is the life that leads to real joy and contentment.

God is not looking for oaths or offerings. In fact, there is nothing we can give him that will help us merit eternal life. God is more interested in what we are willing to let go than what we can offer. Jesus said when we let go of our lives, we will find fulfillment. Matthew 10:39 says, "Whoever finds their life will lose it, and whoever loses their life for my sake will find it." Jesus is telling us to make God's will a priority.

We must surrender to God's purpose even when his desires conflict with our own. As believers, we must accept God's plan rather than seek to satisfy our own ambitions. Not that it's wrong to have plans or make our lives more comfortable. Instead, Jesus is asking that we make God's will our primary concern.

Sometimes, God asks for greater levels of surrender, which often puts us in tough spots. But no matter the strain, God still invites us to follow his path. Acts of obedience certainly help us become more like Christ, but we must recognize that these acts alone don't earn us God's presence. We have God's presence in our hearts because our faith is in Christ.

It's important to understand that the refining process is for growth. However, growth does not question whether we have eternal life. That's because when we are in the purging process, the Spirit is already present in our hearts. And since we already have this life in us, we can find happiness. This means we can delight in God wherever we are in the process. Whether we face difficulties or even experience shortcomings, we can still have joy and fulfillment.

Openness with God Produces Growth

The process of developing character is not always pleasant. Certainly, God will add wisdom, knowledge, and virtue during times of ease. But Christlikeness is developed in unique ways through our trials. For we learn to depend on God during hardships after obedience has been tested. Sure, there are many ways we can show our devotion to God, but allowing him to purge us conveys our ultimate commitment. That's because his purging is thorough, and only growth in Christ is allowed to flourish. We read in Matt 15:13, "Every plant that my heavenly Father has not planted will be pulled up by the roots."

The purging process seeks to uproot anything hindering our growth. Sure, we may not always know what's getting in the way, but God knows the source of our troubles. And once the source has been identified, he uses adversity to remove whatever is stopping us.

We make a mistake when we think adversity is the source of our problems. But adversity isn't the problem. For it merely causes real problems to surface. Ironically, our disappointments, losses, and unanswered prayers may be the very things that bring about lasting change. For God uses these things to do a masterful work. Though we may not understand it now, it will all make sense after the difficulty passes.

A Vision for Complete Happiness

We might wonder why God doesn't respond the way we expect. Or why adversity is allowed to go on while our prayers remain unanswered. These questions are best understood when we realize God has a specific vision for our lives.

It's not that God is being oppositional or ignoring our prayers. Rather, he's helping us stay the course. God is using adversity to guide us to our destiny. And if we allow him to work in our lives, we'll find happiness and fulfillment.

Truly, the vision we have for our lives stops short of complete happiness. When we take control of our own lives, we obtain only a temporary satisfaction that won't endure. However, if we pursue God's vision, we'll be rewarded with eternal life and lasting joy.

God doesn't tell us everything from the beginning. So naturally, we don't fully understand what he's doing when he first starts working in our lives. In fact, it's easy to misunderstand him.

Even though he is masterful at orchestrating our lives, his work doesn't always make sense. That's because he has an eternal perspective. Not only that, but he's also never in a rush and catches every detail. That means nothing will be overlooked or forgotten.

However, God's patience doesn't always seem like an immediate advantage, especially when we're under extreme pressure. But we must learn to trust him even when we don't understand what he's doing.

When we notice God's hand in our lives, we are seeing his vision unfold. And if God is at work, we can be confident he will complete what he started. There is excitement when God is working. Even though we don't know everything he has in store, we know his vision for us is perfect. And when we experience what God has planned, it will bring true happiness and fulfillment.

God Is Perfecting Our Lives

God is skillful in his work and knows how to make masterpieces. This gives us confidence that he can handle every detail of our lives. This means we can let our guard down with him. Sure, we have insecurities, but we don't have to hide anymore. That's because he can be trusted.

Sadly, we grow accustomed to protecting and silencing our true emotions. Since we have learned to neglect these feelings, God will use uncomfortable situations to expose them. So, we must trust that he knows what we need. And even though we must endure discomfort, we know God's peace will be with us.

God perfects the areas of our lives that need refinement and strength. His craftsmanship is flawless. And he doesn't grow tired or leave out details. God is never confused about his vision and never makes mistakes. Truly, we are being perfected by the hand of God.

The finished work of the Father will be a wonder to see. God will look upon the work of his hands and declare that it's good. A vessel made for honor. A masterpiece created in the Son!

Our Hearts Matter

We know God is good and seeks purity in his creation. So, when God looks upon us, he desires to see holiness and righteousness. But heavenly virtues come only by faith in Jesus. And this means we not only believe in Jesus, but we agree to follow a divine vision for our lives.

In Christ, we bring pleasure to the Creator. And even though we might not be perfect, our placement in God's favor doesn't change if our faith is in Jesus. All that matters is that we become more like Christ every day.

However, God already views us perfect in Christ. When God looks at us, he doesn't see our imperfections. Rather, he sees the perfection of Christ. It's not about our stumbling or failure. In fact, God sees us either in Christ or out of his provision for righteousness. And now that we are in Christ, we are positioned in God's grace. What God wants to see now is our growth.

Sure, there are some days we feel more "holy" than on others. That's because God's in the process of perfecting our lives. And even though there's a need for growth, he's still pleased with us. There's no expectation to be perfect. In fact, perfection is not even possible. That's why we needed a Savior. And now, we have Christ's righteousness, and he's already lived a sinless life.

However, God is looking for something else. And what he seeks cannot be given through our own perfection. But if perfection, holiness, and righteousness already belong to God, what could we possibly give him that matters?

God wants our hearts!

He wants our most intimate selves. God wants the part of our lives that we hide from everyone else. He wants to be our God, and for us to be his people. Sure, it may be difficult to let him into these secret areas, but we need to start by giving him what we can.

We give our hearts to God despite our insecurities because we trust him. God knows this trust takes time. And this is the reason he leads us down paths that demonstrate his faithfulness. There is comfort knowing that God is seeking after our hearts. And because he loves us, we can let him into these secret places.

Chapter 10

Jesus Shows Us How to Follow God's Will

GOD LOVED US BEFORE we even thought of loving him. And because of his great love, he took the initial step and provided a way of salvation. God was not reacting to our demands for a savior but was compelled by mercy to meet our need for deliverance.

Even Jesus proved his compassion when he willingly suffered and died for all. Although it was God's will for Jesus to endure the cross, Jesus proved his love by freely offering himself for our forgiveness.

Making God's Will a Priority

Despite what we might think, Jesus's life was not easy.

He endured trials, persecution, and ultimately death. And even though it was difficult at times, Jesus still delighted in God's will. He considered obeying God's will more important than anything else.

Certainly, Jesus was obedient to every word God spoke. But he did not do this grudgingly. Instead, Jesus considered God's will the only priority in his life. Jesus said in John 4:34, "My food . . . is to do the will of him who sent me and to finish his work."

Can we arrive at a place in our lives where obedience is the only priority?

Of course, there is a difference between perfect obedience and prioritizing obedience. We cannot attain perfect obedience. God sent Jesus for this reason. And Jesus provides righteousness for all who believe in him by faith. This righteousness is freely given, perfect, and approved by God. There is nothing we can add to or take away from what Jesus has done.

But when obedience is a priority, we seek to follow the Spirit in all things. And as the Spirit leads us, we strive to keep pace with him through our obedience.

Being able to recognize God's goodness and compassion leads to obedience. And when we understand that God has our best interest in mind, we will want to do what he asks. Sure, there are times when God will request difficult things, but he will never demand anything that will bring us eternal harm. But if we lose sight of God's good nature, we will misunderstand his commitment to our well-being and hesitate to follow his path.

Jesus Is God and His Teachings Are Good

In the story of the rich young ruler (Matt 19:16–26), we see Jesus requesting something difficult.

The Scripture tells us that the young ruler asked Jesus if there was anything he needed to accomplish for eternal life. Jesus's response was not what the young ruler expected. But from the beginning, this young ruler correctly acknowledged that Jesus was a teacher of good things. To this Jesus replied that only God was good.

With Jesus's reply, the young ruler would've had to reconcile his understanding of Jesus with the character of God himself. In other words, to consider the teachings and works of Jesus "good," this young ruler would've had to agree that they were of God.

We are confronted with the same truths today.

It's one thing to consider the teachings and works of Jesus as being "good," but do we recognize them as coming from God? And do we accept Jesus's words as those spoken by God?

The young ruler was given the opportunity to acknowledge that Jesus was, in fact, speaking with the authority of God. Jesus then told the young ruler to keep the commandments and he would have eternal life. Jesus's reply should have helped the young ruler identify his need for mercy, as no one can keep all the commandments.

However, the young ruler responded that he had kept all the commandments since childhood. It seemed like the young ruler was saying he had kept all the commandments and would do anything else required of him to obtain eternal life. Jesus then made a difficult request and told the young ruler to sell his possessions, give to the poor, and follow him. The young ruler couldn't do this and went away sorrowful because he had great wealth.

What was Jesus really doing when he told the young ruler all these things?

We can see that Jesus was giving the young ruler an opportunity to follow God through obedience. Yes, it was a hard thing that Jesus asked, but obedience isn't always easy. Following commandments is different than obeying God. That's what Jesus is trying to get the young ruler to see.

If the young ruler could lay aside the old covenant of laws and learn to obey God, he would be perfect. For the young ruler's obedience would have led him to depend on Jesus for eternal life. And this would have made him perfect.

What God Wants for Us

God's nature is good, and he will continue to perfect our lives through obedience. It's not about how many rules we keep, or which commandments are followed. Rather, it's whether we said "yes" to his will.

We must recognize that God's plan for us is to become more like Christ. First Thessalonians 4:3 says, "It is God's will that you should be sanctified." By this, God has made it clear what he wants for every believer. We are to embrace the refining process and produce spiritual fruit. And when we do this, we are kept in the center of his will.

Trying to Move God

Sometimes, it feels like God withholds blessings from us, especially when we are going through difficult times. It can feel like God is keeping good things from us because of his silence and because our prayers aren't being answered like we think they should be. We know God can help, but we wonder if he's willing to help when we need him most.

We try to persuade him, but our efforts are often misguided. That's because we somehow think our works obligate him to show us favor. But even though our efforts and works are good, they do not cause God to act on our behalf.

There is a right way to view our relationship with God, and it doesn't involve giving him a list of demands. Humility acknowledges that God freely acts out of his own love and isn't under any obligations to us. Yes, we are important in his eyes, but this doesn't mean that he owes us anything or that we can order him around.

We are accustomed to quick fixes and getting our needs met instantly. But, as is no surprise, God doesn't work that way. Sometimes, God will delay responses until we understand his truths or until he has accomplished a work in us. Then he will provide the answers to our prayers.

Although it's important to reach our destiny, God won't rush and overlook the details along the way. But even though he's never in a rush, his timing is always perfect!

Recognizing God as Ruler

Since God is sovereign, we can believe his promises and trust his word. We know God's words are faithful because when he speaks, life springs forth. Just look at what can be seen in creation. It was spoken into existence; and it is currently being upheld by his power. And if creation can rely on him, surely we can depend on his faithfulness too.

Our lives are part of the world God made and we can have confidence knowing he doesn't leave his works incomplete. What has not already been completed will be accomplished in the end. The next time doubt and discouragement start to creep in, all we need to do is look around at creation and remind ourselves that God is faithful.

It's difficult to lay aside personal desires to follow a divine path. But these decisions become easier when we recognize that God is sovereign. Knowing that he is Lord of all things and rightly rules over us helps us willingly surrender to him in love. And when we lay aside personal desires to follow God, we share in Christ's death. So, if we identify with Christ's death, we will experience the joy of life.

We Are Incomplete without Christ

Even though comfort shouldn't dictate our decisions, it's hard to deny that God's plan ultimately gives us peace. We have peace in our trials and peace while we wait for his promises.

There's no need to worry about our journey because God guides us toward fulfillment. And this fulfillment comes from following his plan and being close to him. Truly, wherever God leads, we will find contentment.

The key to contentment in life is understanding that without Christ we can't obtain real peace from our troubles. It's impossible for anything else to provide the comfort we need. The secret is knowing that everything we need comes through the rest we find in Christ.

Jesus was sent to make us whole, and now God seeks to complete this work in our lives. But before we can be made whole and experience God's blessings, we must acknowledge our need for

Christ. Mark 2:17 says, "It is not the healthy who need a doctor, but the sick. I have not come to call the righteous, but sinners."

As we depend on Christ, God will help us develop the virtues that make us complete. If we find ourselves lacking in spiritual character, know that God already desires to help us change. And he will certainly continue the refining process until Christlikeness is formed in our hearts.

We can have confidence that God will finish the work he started. It may not seem like it now, but we are a masterpiece designed by the Creator himself. We may be unrefined in many areas, but that doesn't stop God. He knows what he's doing and is masterful at his craft. But we shouldn't try to get ahead of God and rush the process. All we need to do is trust him and he will get us where we need to be.

Seeking God in Faith during Silent Times

Knowing God is at work doesn't necessarily make the refining process any easier. Sometimes, we experience mixed emotions about what God is doing. And even though we have faith, there can still be frustration and disappointment. But our trust must be firmly placed in him even when we don't know what he is up to.

So, what does it take for God to say we are faithful?

Do we need to remain perfect in every trial, never complaining or stumbling? Or is God looking for something else?

It's a relief to know God doesn't require our perfection. Christ has already accomplished that. What God wants is our faith and trust. Whether giant faith or the smallest amount, God honors our faith.

Sure, he recognizes that some trials are more difficult to endure than others. And that learning to embrace hardships with complete trust takes time. But we can know that when our faith and trust are in him, he's okay with the process.

God provides us with strength to endure every trial. For it's in our weakest moments his strength is revealed. And he promises that we will never be overcome by our troubles if we lean on him.

But there are times when we must search for him, especially when he feels distant. That's why pursuing God when it feels like he has abandoned us is an expression of faith. Yes, we all have experienced his sovereign silence and are often confused about what to do in the quietness. But what we do in these moments defines our character and determines the bond we have with him.

We can choose to doubt God's goodness and turn away from him in unbelief. Or we can follow Jesus's example, who searched after God in faith.

During Jesus's darkest moments, he pursued God. When the heavens went silent, and life was at its worst, Jesus said, "My God, my God, why have you forsaken me?" (Mark 15:34). Jesus searched after God when life couldn't get any worse. And even though God was silent, Jesus still cried out.

We are to follow Jesus's example and chase after God when we feel alone. For our faith is strengthened when we seek after God in the silent times. So, let us be encouraged and know that God never leaves us and will always see our faith.

Having Courage to Face Trials

Faith seems to naturally flow when God fills our lives with ease and comfort. Of course, we need these times to strengthen our relationship. And it's important for us to know that God is not all about trials and difficulty.

In times of blessing, we experience refreshing and restoration. However, faith is tested uniquely when God becomes silent. To experience more satisfaction in life we must learn to search for God when he feels distant. If we start to seek God with all our heart, we will find him. Jeremiah 29:13 says, "You will seek me and find me when you seek me with all your heart."

At times, God seems to remove himself from us so our faith can be strengthened. It may seem like he has abandoned us, but instead he seeks to teach us something. Ironically, this is when we learn God is always with us and never leaves us to face our struggles alone. And it's during the silent times that these truths become real as we search for him in faith.

Sometimes, the silence seems overwhelming. But when we focus on God's faithfulness hope begins to arise. So, trials can be endured with confidence because we know he is paying attention to our problems. But when God feels distant, we can search for him by faith. As we stretch our faith to seek God in the silence, we will find him and experience joy and happiness.

Faith during the Challenge

God wants us to be strengthened by our trials and will use these challenges for our good. Certainly, our faith will be strengthened once we realize how God has helped us come through hardships. But the real purpose of our challenges is to find courage and have faith while we are going through difficulties.

God wants us to have the kind of faith that trusts during trials, rather than simply having confidence once our troubles are over. Sometimes, we embrace God's promises with confidence only to despair when adversity comes. But God wants us to have balance in our lives so we can endure challenges in faith. And since his promises don't change with our circumstances, neither should our faith.

Comforted Because God Is Good

We need to be confident in God's ability to fulfill his promises. Not only is he faithful, but he can also bring every promise to pass at just the right time. In fact, time and circumstance are in his control. Knowing that he is in control of all things brings us comfort. But our hope doesn't depend on whether we find ease in this life. Rather, God's faithfulness serves as the anchor to our hope.

Sometimes, it's only by faith that we know our troubles are working for our good. But this confidence doesn't occur naturally. In fact, it's made from withstanding pressure and enduring adversity. This kind of faith helps us have hope as we wait for God's promises. And it's this kind of faith that helps us believe in his goodness even when we face troubles (Heb 11:1–3).

If emotion and impulses guide our faith, our faith will be unsteady and unpredictable. And if our faith isn't grounded in the truth, circumstances will determine our happiness. This is when we need to remind ourselves of what God has already done. So, by focusing on the truth of God's faithfulness, our hopes can be renewed.

We need to remember God's goodness and how he provided deliverance in the past. Recall the sense of peace when God first drew near at salvation. Remember all the battles won and the victories gained. Don't lose ground! Don't forget how he came through when we needed him! If it's hard to find personal examples, we can see how God was faithful to his followers in the Scripture and know he will do the same for us today.

Not Forgetting the Provider

God will deliver us from all our troubles. The problem is that we forget about his goodness when he does. We forget because we are not focused on him and have become more concerned about temporary comforts (Mark 6:52). But this is not how we should live. Instead, our focus should always be on God and fulfilling his will.

Nothing in God's will is insignificant. That's because we know he does everything with purpose. And when God is working, he will take little things and do the miraculous.

In Exod 14:16, God honored faith and performed a mighty work through Moses when he lifted his staff and the sea divided. There was nothing magical about Moses raising his staff over the sea. But God wanted his people to know him. And the only way they could know him was if they had faith. That's exactly what Moses did. Moses believed, trusted, and obeyed. And just like God did for Moses and the children of Israel, he will be faithful to rescue us from our difficulties. All we must do is trust and believe.

The key is to protect our relationship with God once he sets us free from our burdens. It's easy to forget about God's goodness if we don't stay focused on him. We also drift away when we become less dependent on him for the things we need. Sure, some things we know how to do on our own, but we must continue to follow his will and depend on his provision.

There is nothing wrong with being proud of our own contributions. Truly, taking credit for our own work is not the problem. The real problem is not recognizing God's involvement in meeting our needs. It's not that we need to put ourselves down or feel ashamed. In fact, he's not pleased when we view ourselves with such little value.

The truth is God wants us to see how he provides for our needs every day. Not because he wants a pat on the back, but so we can understand our importance to him and see how committed he is to us. In other words, it's for our good that he provides. And it's for our good that we know him as our provider.

Chapter 11

Fulfillment When Completely Surrendered

A JOYFUL LIFE REALLY doesn't exist without periods of adversity. And of course, it would be wrong to expect that everything would be perfect on this side of heaven. But even though everything can't be perfect, we can still have a life that overflows with happiness when we draw close to God. We draw close by acknowledging his goodness and embracing his ways in every situation. However, if we continue to overlook his goodness and withhold our hearts from him, we will not have true contentment.

Even though we should pursue God with all our heart, we still manage to keep part of it away from him. Sometimes, we do this because we have been hurt and don't trust him with our pain. But God knows when our heart is withdrawn from him. Isaiah 29:13 says, "These people come near to me with their mouth and honor me with their lips, but their hearts are far from me." Despite our insecurities and disappointments, we should always draw close to God by listening to his words and surrendering to his will.

A Divided Heart

We can look for happiness on our own, but nothing satisfies our soul like God. And to have joy and peace, we must stay focused on what he alone provides. Even though it's tempting to go our own way, we must pursue his will so that we are not robbed of joy.

Yes, there are other goals in life worth pursuing but none at the cost of our relationship with God. Any goal worth attaining can be accomplished as we embrace his will. If we can't pursue our dreams and stay connected to him, then we should reconsider our dreams. We must stay focused on what's most important. And that's following God.

In Mark 8:33, Jesus gave us an example of what to do when facing distractions that are not aligned with God's will. When Peter tried to prevent Jesus from being crucified, Jesus said to him, "You do not have in mind the concerns of God, but merely human concerns." This shows us that Jesus always remained focused on God's vision for his life and refused to be turned away from that purpose.

Satisfied with the Creator's Plan

It's not always easy to tell when we have placed our desires above God's plan. For this can happen through small compromises that build over time. And because each compromise seems insignificant, we can become blind to their existence. But then there are times when we outright refuse to follow his will. Sure, we have our reasons. But regardless of the reason, we still have not obeyed God.

So, whether we make small compromises or have completely disregarded his will, the result is always the same: stunted spiritual growth. That means there's an interruption in our spiritual lives when we do not follow God's path. In fact, we only find true satisfaction when we are at the center of his will.

We are happiest when we know God and have accepted his plan for our lives. However, we won't be satisfied if we only recognize him as a distant creator. That's because we continue to live independent from him when he's viewed this way.

In other words, if he's viewed as merely the maker of all things, we may not accept the fact that he has the right to rule over us. Not only has he made all things, but he is also the ruler of all things. And as ruler what he says, we must do.

We must surrender to God as ruler and wait on his provision. Because when we act in self-will, we interfere with his blessings. That means if we become impatient and take control, we are no longer dependent on him. But through self-will, have decided to meet our needs without him. And that gets in the way of God's favor. However, if we want to have true joy, we will welcome his rule over our lives and allow him to meet our needs in his own timing.

Knowing God's Plan Is Wisdom

Having a correct view of God leads to a genuine understanding of the truth. Proverbs 9:10 says, "The fear of the LORD is the beginning of wisdom, and knowledge of the Holy One is understanding." True wisdom helps us understand our lives from God's perspective. When we begin to see our problems clearly, change starts to happen. But without this insight, we cannot find the source of our concerns.

God wants us to have wisdom so we can discern what's truly causing our troubles. Which is often the result of drift in our relationship with him. We read in Jas 1:5, "If any of you lacks wisdom, you should ask God, who gives generously to all without finding fault, and it will be given to you."

God had a close relationship with Adam and Eve in the garden, but this was lost due to their disobedience. Wisdom knows that God's plan is to restore what was lost in the beginning. And a true understanding of God's divine purpose recognizes that all along he intended to draw us to Christ through mercy.

God's original creation was divine, holy, and good. There was nothing that could be improved upon. It was a masterpiece. The only thing remaining for Adam and Eve was to walk in relationship with God and follow his will. But they didn't obey God and eventually hid themselves because of their disobedience. All was lost. But what Adam failed to do in the garden, Christ fulfilled on the cross at Calvary.

Since the beginning, starting with Adam, God weaved his plan of redemption throughout history, bringing Christ into the world at precisely the right time. Even now, God seeks to bring restoration and salvation to the world. Wisdom helps us understand that God's plan is to restore all things through Christ. "For as in Adam all die, so in Christ all will be made alive" (1 Cor 15:22).

We Are Complete in Christ

It's easy to acknowledge God's love, but there's a difference when we get to experience it. In fact, he made a way for us to experience his affection every day. First, God restored our relationship by sending a Savior. This allows us to have fellowship. And second, he draws us to himself by making us more like Christ. This is so we can be one (John 17:21–23).

Sure, promises, provision, and prosperity are all important ways God shows us he cares. But he's more concerned about helping us grow in Christ. All these other things are meant to support that purpose. Ephesians 2:10 says, "For we are God's handiwork, created in Christ Jesus." This demonstrates God's continued love for us through Christ.

Not only are we a work created in love, but we also have been given righteousness in Christ through faith. We see this in Phil 3:9, "not having a righteousness of my own that comes from the law, but that which is through faith in Christ—the righteousness that comes from God on the basis of faith." We deserved judgment, but God gave mercy. And instead of casting us aside, he made a way back to him. So, as we continue in faith, we will become more like Christ.

God helps us grow so we can be "complete in Christ" (Col 1:28). Truly, he doesn't want any of us to feel inadequate. Instead, he wants us to possess all the promises in Christ. Some promises we receive now, but others we must wait for until Jesus comes again to reign.

Since God wants to show us his favor, he will remove anything stopping the flow of heavenly blessings. The good news is we don't have to worry about our shortcomings stopping God's plan. That's because he knows how to get us to our destiny and bring us all the promises found in Christ.

God Is Pleased When We Surrender

What's interesting is God's idea of "complete" looks different than what we think. That's because God sees what's in the heart. First Samuel 16:7 says, "The LORD does not look at the things people look at. People look at the outward appearance, but the LORD looks at the heart."

Yes, God considers us complete in Christ even though we have shortcomings. We must remember God isn't looking for perfection. What he seeks is sincere faith and someone who prioritizes obedience (Mark 12:44).

God is challenging us to lay aside our lives for Christ and become light in the world. But sometimes, we become too comfortable with our Christian lifestyle. We get trapped into thinking everything about our lives must always stay nice and neat. Early in our journey, comfort may be helpful. But now, Jesus is asking us to let go of luxuries and give him our all. He is asking that we lay aside our conveniences and pick up our cross.

Sometimes, we do things our way to soften God's demands or to make his will more tolerable. But when we're in control, we aren't relying on God. Truly, he wants to push us out of our comfort zone to where he's in control. And when he's in control, his demands can only be met through faith, trust, and obedience.

But we can't reach this place with God when our cross is made easy to carry by doing things our way. It's not that he wants us to suffer; instead he wants us in a place of surrender. For the burdens we must shoulder can lead us to greater dependence. But when we resist this call to surrender, it prevents us from experiencing growth and fulfillment.

Our Flaws Don't Prevent God's Blessings

Even though we may not be asked to perform great feats or give up everything we own, God does require absolute devotion. This may seem a little daunting right now, but don't worry. He will help us overcome these fears.

Just know that we can never go wrong when we place our trust in God. In fact, he will always show his strength when we need him most. This means we can rely on him to get us through every situation. Thankfully, he comforts us as we go through the tough times. And when God is at work, we will find joy and fulfillment.

We are reminded of God's faithfulness when we think about how we overcame our challenges in the past. And remembering his faithfulness inspires confidence and trust. But even though past experiences have helped us grow closer to God, nothing is more important than trusting him right now. If we can be with God, in this moment, nothing will be too difficult to face. This is because God will take over and fight our battles.

It's good to know that our limitations do not stop God from fulfilling his promises. But sometimes, when we trust God with our now moments, doubt and fear can arise. And although these doubts and fears cause us problems, they don't stop God's plan. For God knows how to get us to our destiny.

We need to face trials with courage. And we can have courage because we know God is with us in the struggle. Recognizing he is with us right now gives us a unique perspective. What that means is our focus should be on his strength and abilities and not our own.

Certainly, this is true freedom. Once our attention is fixed solely on him, we will find encouragement and learn to say with Mary, "the Mighty One has done great things for me—holy is his name" (Luke 1:49).

Didn't Invite the Trouble

God wants us to grow accustomed to his deliverance (Luke 1:74).

Even though it's wise to avoid hardships whenever possible, we don't have to worry whether God will be faithful when we do face them. Now, we don't want to invite problems, but avoiding challenges isn't the path toward real growth. Yes, life is easier when we're not pressed by adversity. But this may not be what's best for us. For we grow when our faith is being stretched. We grow because we learn that God helps us through our challenges.

God wants us to have the inheritance he has provided through Christ (Luke 4:18–19). We are promised blessings, but we must do our part by acting responsibly. Certainly, there are times when we just can't prevent struggles from happening. We try to manage distress, but it doesn't seem like we can do enough to avoid crises. In times like this, we don't have to fear because God has promised to deliver us from our troubles.

God Is Pleased with Progress

God is patient and gives us time to learn from our experiences. As Christlikeness is developed, we discover new, godly reactions to adversity. And this spiritual character always results in honor when it's tested.

First Peter 1:6–7 says, "In all this you greatly rejoice, though now for a little while you may have had to suffer grief in all kinds of trials. These have come so that the proven genuineness of your faith—of greater worth than gold, which perishes even though refined by fire—may result in praise, glory and honor when Jesus Christ is revealed."

When Christlike virtues are present, we feel proud about our responses to life's challenges. Though developing heavenly qualities takes time, we start experiencing growth the moment we surrender to God.

We come to God broken and in need, but over time, he puts the pieces of our lives back together. And because we are grateful for his work, our love for him becomes the highest priority.

It's no longer about how we appear to others or what they think, but about pleasing him. Even if we have difficulty facing challenges, other people's opinions should not distract us from what's most important. Sure, we are accountable, but God's approval is most important. Our focus shouldn't be on impressing people. Instead, we must give our full attention to how God is developing Christlike character in our lives.

We find fulfillment as God molds us into the image of Christ. And it's in this process that we experience true joy. For there's happiness and peace when God approves of the growth in our lives. Even when we struggle, if God is pleased with our progress, that will be enough to bring satisfaction.

There may be pressure from others to grow faster, but this only leads to frantic efforts and self-reliant behavior. However, God wants us to depend on him every step of the way. Not advancing ahead or falling behind, but being present with him, in this moment. That's when we learn to rely on God's strength and follow as he leads.

No Backing Out on Our Commitment to God

Trials can get to the best of us; just look at Job. He was a righteous man and was greatly troubled by his situation (Job 3). God understands that our challenges are difficult. But he also knows they are meant for our eternal good. So, if we rely on him to get us through our troubles, he will be faithful to provide the strength we need to endure. And even when nothing seems to be changing, we must trust and believe that God is still at work.

Trusting God means having confidence he will provide everything we need, especially during tough times. We should have faith like Job that, no matter what happens, our trust will be in God. We see this in Job 13:15, "Though he slay me, yet will I hope in him." That means there's no backing out on God. It also means we accept all things from him, whether they be blessings or trials. For a heart that is willing to embrace all that God offers will be happy and fulfilled.

Chapter 12

Pursuing God in Faith

SERVING GOD WITH ALL our hearts leads to happiness and fulfillment. But we must be careful not to let circumstances or emotion drive our devotion. Instead, our love must be based on commitment and truth. This means we serve God when we're happy and when things aren't going our way. And when we're committed like that, blessings will follow.

Trusting God is always the right choice. For he empowers us to succeed through faith. And because we live by faith, our lives stand out. Yes, there is something different about us. In other words, our lives look different from those who don't trust God. We are unique since we can overcome every challenge with joy. That's because we don't approach challenges the way the world does. The way we approach troubles is to overcome them by faith in God alone.

However, this dependence doesn't put us at a disadvantage. In fact, living by faith is really an advantage because faith is never overlooked or brushed aside. For our faith draws God close. And when he's close, we have peace knowing he will fight our battles. As we draw near, others will see us overcome with joy and find hope for their struggles. Luke 11:33 says, "No one lights a lamp and puts it in a place where it will be hidden, or under a bowl. Instead they put it on its stand, so that those who come in may see the light."

Importance of Living by Faith

As we grow in the refining process, we learn to see our circumstances differently. We see life being centered on God's faithfulness and not on how we feel. We know growth is occurring when we no longer doubt his promises. Instead, we wait in faith to see how his plan will unfold.

When we think about it, it makes sense why God would want us to live by faith. It's really the best way his strength and salvation could be revealed to a lost world. That's because faith is attainable for anyone, therefore making all welcome.

Although all are welcome, God looks for open hearts willing to follow his plan. All we need to do is make room for him. And we make room for him by trusting and believing.

Sure, there will be times when it feels like he's not there. That's when we must continue to trust and believe. For faith helps us trust in God when he feels distant. Of course, he is still with us when there is silence. But it appears that God remains silent at times so that our faith can resound, and we can emerge in strength.

God's Ways Are Different than Our Own

We often lose sight of God's comfort when we face difficult challenges. But instead of feeling overwhelmed, he wants us to have peace. And to have peace we must trust him. However, this becomes more complicated when we are emotionally wounded. Really, it's hard to trust when we are hurting. That's because when we are hurting, we try to protect ourselves. And anything that could potentially harm us gets pushed away. Sadly, we sometimes view God's process as something that is harmful and needs to be pushed away.

A life of faith takes us down tough paths. And these paths teach us a lot about ourselves. But we must know God is at work in the adversity. However, if we view his work as harmful, we might push him away. And when we push God away, it becomes difficult to trust him. What's interesting is the more we choose to trust despite our hurt, the more our hearts embrace the tough paths. But even though God's path doesn't always make sense to us, when we choose to trust, understanding his ways gets easier.

Jesus Is Our Example

We start to understand God's ways a little more as we become like Jesus. We also draw comfort from knowing more about Jesus's nature and his earthly experiences. That's because Jesus's life provides an example of what to do when we are faced with challenges.

So, when we can't see God in our trials, we can look to Jesus. For Jesus showed us how to search in faith when God is silent and how to endure trials in trust when we are weak. On this side of heaven, we never get to see God completely. But he reveals himself by helping us to understand Jesus. We see this in John 1:18, "No one has ever seen God, but the one and only Son, who is himself God and is in closest relationship with the Father, has made him known."

We Try to Understand

It may seem like God is disconnected from us, but despite these feelings we must trust that he cares and will not leave us to face challenges on our own. When it feels like God is distant, faith begins to look for him. But sometimes, our search for God raises more questions than answers.

We can start to wonder, "Why would God ever allow these things to happen to me if I am following his will?"

Sure, it's hard to know what God is doing at times. But that's why we look to Jesus to understand God's nature. For Jesus proved that God is faithful and can always be trusted, even when we face hardships.

When we are not sure what to do, following Jesus is always the right option. We find ourselves in the perfect will of God as we become more like Christ. Even though we may not be able to comprehend the wisdom of the Father, we can certainly follow the example given by the Son.

How to Live by Faith

Jesus asked us to follow him and gave us an example of what it means to live by faith. He even showed us how to endure challenges and remain faithful. So, we can connect with Jesus since he knows what it's like to experience trials. Hebrews 4:15 says, "For we do not have a high priest who is unable to empathize with our weaknesses, but we have one who has been tempted in every way, just as we are—yet he did not sin."

Jesus understands our troubles because he was also immersed into adversity. When our challenges become too great and we don't know what to do, we can follow Jesus's example. He will guide us through every situation and get us through all our troubles.

Our Commitment

Satisfaction in life occurs when we embrace what God has revealed through Jesus. This means we don't look for other explanations of the truth or seek alternatives to God's will. We don't need these because Jesus gave us an example of how we are to live. Even though we can't fully comprehend God's eternal ways, we can know what has been revealed to us through Jesus. Sure, Jesus's sayings can be challenging at times, but we still must fully embrace his truths. And by accepting Jesus's words, we accept the source of his message.

Lack of commitment to Jesus hinders our relationship with God. Even though it may be convenient to pursue comfort and ease, we are asked instead to follow Jesus regardless of the cost.

Jesus instructs us to abandon self-reliance and surrender to God's will. At first, total surrender doesn't seem like such a hard thing, but it gets more difficult as faith is tested. Jesus placed following God's will as the highest priority in life. He said in Matt 4:4, "Man shall not live on bread alone, but on every word that comes from the mouth of God." So, we should also follow Jesus's example and fulfill God's plan in our lives every day.

What It Cost to Follow Jesus

God knows our love for him is sincere, but loving him is only the beginning. We must show our love by laying aside our lives for his purpose. Of course, learning to surrender is not an easy process, but once we do, it brings happiness and fulfillment.

Sometimes, we are reluctant to surrender. But ironically, this can be a good sign. For we should count the cost of following Jesus and either accept or reject him with complete understanding (Luke 14:26–33).

Jesus must be served knowing that our will must submit to God's will. It's important to know the full costs of these decisions. The reason is because we are not permitted to partially embrace Christ just so things will be easy. Instead, we are asked to pursue him in total surrender.

Jesus fully reflects God's nature and reveals his eternal ways. To reject any part of Jesus is to reject God. In the beginning of our Christian journey, when our hearts freely accepted Jesus, we said "yes" to God. Refusing to follow any of Jesus's teachings now is disobedience to God himself.

The point is this: if we want to live with joy and happiness, we must embrace everything Jesus has instructed. This does not mean we have to be perfect. Rather, we need to welcome the words of Christ and allow them to change our lives.

Living like Christ means we choose to depend on God's provision. Part of this provision is helping us delight in laying aside self-will. This tells us that being in the refiner's fire doesn't have to be a negative experience.

We can have joy even as trials shape our lives. In fact, the refining process brings fulfillment when character starts to form in our hearts. But even when it seems like progress is not being made, we still have joy because we know God is always at work. We just need to keep our faith in him and let his plan unfold.

Sometimes, we give up when our circumstances don't improve. And although it's difficult, we can still draw close. The truth is we should always have faith. Of course, this is tough to do when things aren't getting any better.

But regardless of the challenges we face, we should never give up on God. That doesn't mean we will feel better just because we believe. For there are times when we draw near that our faith is still mixed with fear, desperation, and doubt. So, when this happens, we must continue to seek God even if our faith seems weakened by our troubles.

Cleansed from Everything Hidden in the Heart

Once we realize that we are safe with God, we can willingly surrender. And when we surrender, he cleanses us of everything that displeases him (Ps 51). Even if we've made mistakes, God provides a way for us to become pure. For Christ purifies our minds and frees us from guilt.

We read in Heb 9:14, "How much more, then, will the blood of Christ, who through the eternal Spirit offered himself unblemished to God, cleanse our consciences from acts that lead to death, so that we may serve the living God!" Now, we are free from shame, and God's presence fills our hearts. This is his process at work helping us draw near with a clean conscience.

Being Connected

Our relationship with God must overshadow any difficulty we face. Because in the end, it's not about whether we "aced the test," but about the connection we've made with him. Did we draw closer? Did we learn more about him? Did we share his love? We need to focus on what really matters. And that's our nearness to God.

We are guided down paths that bring fulfillment as we follow God. Truly, our lives are enriched at every step through the process because of his care. But we can only please him if we remain in his refining process. And even though we have imperfections and shortfalls, God is still satisfied with us because we are growing in Christ. John 3:21 says, "But whoever lives by the truth comes into the light, so that it may be seen plainly that what they have done has been done in the sight of God."

The Great Exchange

So many things try to distract us from making God a priority, but nothing brings happiness like following his will. He has our eternal well-being in mind and knows how to bless his followers.

Those that abandon self-reliance know they can depend on God. But even though we abandon worldly pursuits, we can still have satisfaction in life. For it's never considered a loss to make sacrifices for the kingdom. A far greater reward than could ever be imagined is obtained simply by surrendering. There is also more satisfaction in what is received than what is lost. For we lay aside doubt and pick up life, and we surrender self and inherit the everlasting God. It is evident that we are the ones benefiting most from this generous exchange!

Our lives are better off when we abandon everything for God. There's no need to hold back to protect possessions or guard against insecurities. True happiness and joy occur when we surrender everything to him. Sure, our basic needs must be addressed to function in this world, but these alone cannot satisfy.

The pleasures of this world are temporary and last only for a short time. Eventually this type of fulfillment fades, but the satisfaction we have in God never ends. Jesus said in John 4:14, "But whoever drinks the water I give them will never thirst. Indeed, the water I give them will become in them a spring of water welling up to eternal life."

Reflecting Christ in Every Circumstance

No matter what challenges may come our way, we can still experience joy. This is because satisfaction in life doesn't come from external possessions or favorable circumstances. These things really don't lead to happiness. In fact, peace and joy are the result of spiritual growth. And spiritual growth happens when we become more like Christ through the refining process.

We must trust that God will use our challenges to bring about eternal good. This doesn't mean it will always be pleasant, fair, or easy. It simply means, from an eternal perspective, it will be what's best for us. However, God is not only considering us in the trial. He is also looking to influence others through our difficulties. Much of the adversity we endure not only results in personal growth but turns out to be an encouragement to others.

We are to display Christ in this world. And the knowledge people have about Jesus, they often see in his followers. Whose thoughts do we reflect in our adversity? Whose character do we reveal in our success? Whose nature do we portray in our relationships? We have a responsibility to show spiritual virtues so people can see and learn of Christ.

The truth is God wants us to become good witnesses so other people can see Jesus in us. Matthew 5:16 says, "Let your light shine before others, that they may see your good deeds and glorify your Father in heaven." That's the mission. But our lives are to be eclipsed by Christ's so that others will only recognize him. That means we should be less concerned about our comfort and more concerned about growing in Christ. Then our light will shine bright to bring hope and encouragement to others.

Chapter 13

No Longer Looking for an Escape

THERE ARE TIMES WHEN it seems like there is no end to our distress. Just know, God's sustaining grace is enough. He can help us overcome anything we face. So, instead of escaping our challenges, God invites us to draw strength from him so we can endure them.

However, turning away from God during difficult times separates us from the only source of true comfort. And when we become bitter against God's process, it prevents us from receiving healing and deliverance. Sure, there are times when we just want trials to end. But if God chooses not to remove our troubles, then he will be sure to give enough strength for the journey.

Our spiritual development is interrupted when we stop living by God's strength. But the way of grace is the only path that equips us for his purpose. This means we can't fulfill our destiny without totally depending on God. Even cutting the refining season short will leave our growth stunted and out of balance. And if trials are avoided, we will not be able to fulfill our destiny. So, instead of asking God to stop trials, we should run to him and find the comfort and strength we need to endure.

When we feel like there is too much pressure in life, we naturally want these experiences to end. But God allows us to be in these situations to test our faith. It may seem like we can't make it through at times, but we must remember God will help us overcome every challenge.

We Desire God's Blessings

We don't always see clearly in our weakest moments. Trials can be so difficult at times that finding rest seems hopeless. So, we start to assume God doesn't want us to have comfort. Our faith gets shaken, and we become blind to his goodness. Then once we realize he has allowed these difficulties but has not explained his reasons for the hardships, doubt and negative emotions begin to surface.

But if we take a closer look, we find that our real desire is not necessarily for these circumstances to change. What we want is for God to give his promised blessings. We are not merely looking to get our way. Our desire is to have his acceptance, approval, and favor.

It can appear to us like endless trials are God's way of showing disapproval. Sometimes, we think he's purposely withholding blessings, especially when he seems so distant.

Sure, we don't deserve God's goodness. But the truth is, Christ provided a way for us to obtain favor through faith. So, we are blessed in Christ even when our circumstances say something different.

God Has a Purpose for the Test

When trials persist, we must examine our lives to see if there is anything that would cause God to lift his favor. If there is no cause for disapproval, then we must accept his sovereign will and trust he has a purpose in the test.

Many times, he uses trials to separate us from empty pursuits. That's because we don't know what it takes to live a fulfilled life and are often distracted by self-will. But his process seeks to reveal and provide for our greatest need. And to fulfill our deepest needs, we are asked to trust God's provision. When we embrace

God's process, we will have satisfaction in life. But resisting trials and avoiding adversity will not bring the fulfillment we seek (Job 13:20–21).

We must remind ourselves that God is not ignoring our prayers by his silence. Instead, he is acting in our best interest. And though our circumstances may not make sense now, they will, in time. Even Job's affliction turned out to be a bigger blessing in the end. Job did not have a clue what awaited him while he was in the middle of his suffering, but God knew. God also planned that Job's troubles would bring comfort and encouragement to many that would eventually hear his story.

When we love and trust God, our hearts run in the direction he has chosen. We learn to embrace his work even if his hand is pressing heavily upon us. But just because we follow his will doesn't mean our challenges are any easier to cope with. In fact, our challenges continue to be obstacles in our path.

Even though it seems overwhelming at times, our trust must remain in God. And as we stop hiding from his process and start embracing what he has planned, we find happiness, peace, and joy.

Our Effort to Surrender

We do not fade in and out of Christ but are always immersed in his grace. And if we stay committed in faith, God approves us. Even when he is silent and troubles persist, our position in Christ stays secure. It doesn't matter whether there are slips or stumbling; we remain in Christ if we continue to believe.

It's easy to get disappointed when our character does not reflect Christ's nature. Yes, sometimes, the old self gets in the way even though our heart's true desire is to be like Jesus. However, it's important not to lose sight of what God values. God values our dependence on him. Surely, God is not impressed by our strength or abilities. What he wants is for us to rely on his strength.

God's strength is often revealed in our weakness. But just because we have a negative reaction to a trial doesn't mean God has stopped working in our lives. We begin to lose focus when we think God expects perfection from us. In fact, God has made it clear that he is more interested in our ability to surrender.

Trust Causes Growth to Happen

We develop real happiness when we trust God. Truly, the decision to trust is an act of faith. Not only is trust an act of faith, but it is also the reason why growth occurs. In other words, growth doesn't happen because we've successfully accomplished a task for God. Instead, growth happens because we surrendered our hearts and trusted him to make a way through our trials.

God is not asking for grand gestures. He simply asks us to trust him. No, we are not aiming to get everything right. Our goal is to please him. And we please him with faith and trust. So, when we live with faith and trust, we have happiness and fulfillment.

We must remember that God is in the process of making our lives reflect his glory, and this process takes time. Certainly, he will extend mercy when we stumble; all we need to do is ask. And because he is patient and understanding, our shortcomings will not deter him from completing his work.

Our Weaknesses Help Us

We may think our weaknesses jeopardize the plan of God, but these can be catalysts for our success. What we esteem as a detriment to our lives God can use to fulfill our destiny. Now, this doesn't mean we will never have to change our ways. Quite the opposite. God will refine our weaknesses until they can be used for his purpose.

God will use our perceived weaknesses to help us accomplish great things. On our own, these weaknesses are limitations, but with God anything becomes possible. But our focus must be on God's ability, not on our own imperfections. For we must start to believe we are complete in Christ. And because we are kept by God's power, we can boldly say, "I am an overcomer!" (1 Pet 1:5).

Being kept by God's power means we are surrounded by his presence. And in his presence, we have everything we need to live a satisfying life. Things outside of God's presence are temporary and do not bring fulfillment. This tells us that even our circumstances have not escaped his control. The truth is he may use what causes us discomfort to bring about the greatest blessings. For this reason, resilience is part of his plan.

Hearing and Seeing to Obey

We see God drawing people to himself throughout generations. And today he is bringing us close through Christ. Knowing what God has done in the past to bring us to Christ assures us that he is not going to neglect his plan for us now (John 1:1–18).

God watches over us carefully and wants to be involved in our lives. First Peter 3:12 says, "For the eyes of the Lord are on the righteous and his ears are attentive to their prayer." This lets us know that we have God's full attention. Our part is to let everything of insignificance fade and focus only on what is important.

The relationship we have with God must be our top priority. But it can be difficult to focus on God when we are only concerned about finding relief from our troubles. Sure, it's important to be comfortable, but this should never take the place of a surrendered heart.

Sometimes, we can get so worried about getting through a challenge that we miss what God is saying. Instead, we should listen for God's voice despite our distress. And when he speaks, we should be ready not only to hear but to obey as well. That's because we learn how to adequately handle our challenges through obedience. Sure, his ways seem unusual at first, but they ultimately lead us to victory. Therefore, we must be sensitive to God's leading, so we know which path to follow.

Being Easily Guided

We must follow God if we want to experience an abundant life. That's because experiencing an abundant life is the result of living in the Spirit. But the Spirit is not forceful with his guidance. For he speaks when we are still. That means our hearts must be quiet. Through humility and obedience, we can quiet ourselves before God. And this ensures that we do not interrupt the work of the Spirit (1 Thess 5:19).

Real change occurs when we take a close look at ourselves and choose to act in obedience. Taking an honest look means we leave no room for manipulation with God. In other words, we do not try to bargain with him or talk our way out of what he is saying. We know when he speaks and his words are final.

The refining process teaches us not to wrestle against God, especially when his words make us uncomfortable. For he wants us to be easily guided. But if we cannot hear him, distractions may have distorted his voice. And if his voice is distorted, distractions must be removed so we can fulfill our destiny.

God Is in Our Future

It's hard to accept that we cannot reflect Christ's nature on our own. But truthfully, our efforts and abilities do not help us look like Jesus. For these virtues are developed only by the Spirit. That means our boast cannot be in ourselves, but in God who is performing a great work in us. And because he is doing this work, it brings us encouragement and hope. Second Thessalonians 2:16–17 says, "May our Lord Jesus Christ himself and God our Father, who loved us and by his grace gave us eternal encouragement and good hope, encourage your hearts and strengthen you in every good deed and word."

The path we travel is not necessarily an easy one. Because on this journey we experience both blessing and adversity. However, through it all we can have happiness. We don't have to worry about tomorrow. For no matter how far into the future we gaze, God is there to provide for our needs. Even if we only have a little hope, we'll find the strength to make it through. This is because God remains faithful to his promises and will not leave us.

There is hope for tomorrow because God will be there to give us strength. His power keeps us from falling and ensures we are never overtaken in our difficulties. Instead of being overtaken, we learn valuable lessons from the trials we encounter. We learn to be more like Jesus and become vessels that God can use for his purpose. Also, embracing God's work in our lives enables us to bring comfort and encouragement to others.

Prepared for the Kingdom

Improving our relationship with God causes us to have a greater impact in the world. He wants us to make a difference and will do mighty things through us even if we only have a few talents. There is much we can do for the kingdom. All God is looking for is sincere faith and a willing heart so he can reveal his power.

But only what we offer God with a surrendered heart benefits his kingdom. As we surrender, he works through us to do mighty things. When he reaches through us to influence our world, we experience fulfillment. For it brings true happiness when he moves through us to bring someone else hope and encouragement. And by bringing someone hope and encouragement we are performing God's work.

Truly, there is no greater joy than knowing we are fit for his purpose. Second Timothy 2:21 states, "Those who cleanse them-selves . . . will be instruments for special purposes, made holy, use-ful to the Master and prepared to do any good work."

The refining process keeps us ready to fulfill God's will. That means we should always wait with a quiet heart. We wait quietly so we can hear what he is saying. He will guide us, but we must be sensitive and keep pace. This is what allows him to work in our lives. But this process takes time and can't be rushed. And even though we can't rush the process, we can become more attentive to him today by quieting our hearts.

Our ears learn to listen, and our eyes learn to see when we embrace God's path. But whatever he says we must be willing to do. If we are willing to obey, he will prepare us for where he leads. And because our confidence and trust are in God, we will be secure in his hands. This is what leads to satisfaction in life.

Chapter 14

Having Confidence in God

GOD ASKS US TO have faith as we push through our challenges. Even though this can be difficult, we learn to move forward in obedience despite our troubles. Just like in the Scripture, it probably didn't make sense when the feeble man heard Jesus say, "Get up and walk." But this man did not let his challenges and limitations stop him from obeying. And so, by faith he followed Jesus's voice and did the impossible (John 5:8).

Sometimes, God asks that we use our faith to push past our troubles. That doesn't mean that we simply believe for God to deliver us from momentary distress. Rather, it means having confidence that he will empower us to accomplish his plan no matter how challenging it becomes.

It's encouraging to know that God invites us to place our burdens upon him. But what's interesting is handing our burdens over to God doesn't require any strength. Quite the opposite. In fact, it requires all the weakness we can muster. We are to become vulnerable with him and trust he will protect us.

Yes, he knows exposing our weaknesses is difficult for us. That's why letting go of our troubles is an act of faith. We honor God when we let our guard down and allow him to defend our hearts. We read in Ps 55:22, "Cast your cares on the LORD and he will sustain you; he will never let the righteous be shaken."

The Little Things Seem to Matter the Most

Sometimes, it seems easier to do a difficult thing for God than to obey him in a small thing. But it's through these small things that he performs great works. To resolve our challenges, he may ask us to perform simple tasks that appear completely unrelated to our problem. At first, what God is asking doesn't seem to directly address our concerns. However, it's through these small acts of obedience that we find healing and growth.

We may think that daily struggles contribute little to our success as a believer, but it's in these battles we learn trust and obedience. For it's in the simple things we take for granted that God does his greatest work.

Agreeing to do great things for God is impressive, but it really pleases him when we are obedient in the small things. Through ordinary, everyday events we learn the invaluable principles of love, integrity, and faithfulness. These qualities are developed through the Spirit using ordinary circumstances. Truly, God's lessons are near us every day.

In fact, his refining work is being done right now in our current situation. We do not need grand displays of power or mighty miracles to experience his work. It occurs in the middle of everyday life. The mundane and routine occurrences in our lives become God's purging ground.

Help to Handle the Stress

We can rely on God to deliver us from our struggles when faced with stress. Yes, he knows routine situations give us trouble and recognizes that we get overwhelmed at times. And while some events cause more stress than others, build-up from the "daily grind" is what affects us most. We get strain from everyday living and need help from God to adequately deal with these problems.

Having confidence in God means we don't have to stress out about the little things. When we experience daily struggles, it's important to ask ourselves, "What's God trying to show me?"

Often, there is a bigger lesson to learn as we endure our difficulties. Through it all, we should be open to what God is doing in our lives. Sometimes, we may feel our stress is impossible to overcome or that we can't go on. But if God says we can overcome, we can!

Facing the "daily grind" may seem overwhelming, but with God we can achieve anything. Sometimes, there doesn't seem to be an end to all the demands on our time and energy. But when we feel depleted, our rest can be found in Jesus. In him, there is strength for every day if we continue to trust and believe. We don't need to worry about where strength for tomorrow will come from. For we should only focus on what is needed right now. Take one day at a time. This day, this moment!

Though we may feel overwhelmed and unable to carry on, we can rely on God to help us tolerate the stress. He can help us endure everyday situations with joy and patience. It's easy to think that the most extreme challenges pose the greatest risk to our faith, but it seems that the routine stresses of life tend to pull us away from God's promises more than anything else.

Our hope needs to be so firmly placed in his promises that it cannot be shaken by any difficulty or challenge. And no matter what happens, we should always anticipate God working in our situation. We can rejoice when facing every trial because he's always moving on our behalf.

Waiting on God's Plan to Unfold

If we know anything about God, it's that he has immeasurable love for his people. And this endless and faithful compassion is the reason why we can rely on him. As we grow in the Lord our expectations begin to change. Initially, we want God to step in and resolve all our problems. But as growth occurs, we become more concerned about his plan than our personal comfort.

It is written in Rom 5:3–5, "But we also glory in our sufferings, because we know that suffering produces perseverance; perseverance, character; and character, hope. And hope does not put us to shame, because God's love has been poured out into our hearts through the Holy Spirit." Whether mundane experiences or great challenges, we know it's all part of a greater purpose.

The steps toward accomplishing God's plan are not always easy and we often make our fair share of mistakes. But each step brings us closer to God. Even when it looks like nothing is happening, we have hope that God is still moving. Romans 8:24 says, "But hope that is seen is no hope at all." It may not feel like God is working at times, but he uses the silence to draw us to his promises. We must recognize that each trial and difficulty are part of his process.

His Leading Will Strengthen Our Faith

We don't have to worry about how our circumstances will turn out. Though we hope for positive results, our trust must remain in God regardless of the outcome. No matter what he has planned for us, we can be content, and that brings comfort.

When we walk in step with God, we are naturally drawn into his will. This frees us from being overly concerned about things. We have confidence because we know our trials have already been accounted for in his plan. So, we must trust that he wants to guide us to an eternal reward, and that he alone knows how to help us reach our destiny. And with him as our guide, we know that he will handle what is beyond our control.

Enduring hardships with peace and joy is essential for believers. But this is not accomplished because of our many talents. Only God can help us express this Christlike character. So, we must always be mindful of what God wants rather than focusing on our difficult circumstances. When we focus on what God is doing, it helps us follow wherever he leads.

Certainly, God can lead us into difficult situations. But the purpose of these trials is to strengthen our faith. We must know that if he is leading us into these places, peace will accompany the process. Peace may not occur immediately, but after God completes his work, we will experience rest.

A Greater Purpose for Our Troubles

We may not associate having peace and joy with God's power, but truly this is some of his finest work. Taking someone from panic to peace and from sorrow to stillness is a mighty work of the Spirit. Nothing or no one can comfort our hearts like the Holy Spirit.

When we suffer tragedy or distress, it is not material things that bring the most encouragement, it's God's presence. When he brings comfort, nothing else is necessary. Right in the middle of our distress we can be comforted by his presence. And when he is with us, we can rest in his peace.

We can have comfort even if our circumstances do not change. The only thing we need is God to be with us in the trial. For he empowers us to do what's right and brings peace when we face troubles. And because he's near, we have strength for the journey.

Sometimes, we get confused and think God is somehow to blame for everything. But in the end, this thinking does not bring peace. What brings confidence is understanding that nothing will disrupt his plan for our lives. Circumstances that are out of our control are not too difficult for God. And if he chooses not to re-move a problem, then there must be an eternal purpose for it.

Even though we may not see how it will all work out, God can still be trusted. He has been carrying out his plan for a long time and knows what he's doing. Sure, our situation may be tough, but his path ultimately ends in our comfort. He even helps us experi-ence a small piece of heavenly rest during our stay here on earth. Truly, we have a peace that is beyond understanding (Phil 4:7) and a joy that is beyond description (1 Pet 1:8).

Not a Common Response

We provide a yielded life, but God creates virtue and growth. The virtues of happiness, peace, and joy cannot be obtained without his presence in our lives. It's only his power that can help us rise above common responses to hardships. Instead of responses like distress and despair, we can have peace and comfort in Christ (2 Cor 4:7–10).

Sometimes, we stop relying on God as the source of our strength and try to endure trials alone. This can prove to be an extremely difficult way to approach challenges. Even though we are strong, the pressure can become too great at times. And because we are not resting in him, our peace gets disrupted. Also, if we grow impatient and are reluctant to follow him, we can become discouraged when trials persist. But staying obedient in faith helps us remain in his peace. And this allows him to accomplish his work through our trials.

God Helps Us through This Journey

God preserves our joy and provides comfort even in times when we feel faint. Sometimes, it seems like God takes the long way around, but he knows just how to help us. That's because we don't always know what we need. Surprisingly, what we think is best for our lives, God knows will not be enough.

It may not seem possible now, but we can have joy in our trials. There is joy because we know God is using our challenges to help us get to our destiny. But we can only have fulfilling lives if we follow his path. Second Corinthians 4:16–18 says,

> Therefore we do not lose heart. Though outwardly we are wasting away, yet inwardly we are being renewed day by day. For our light and momentary troubles are achieving for us an eternal glory that far outweighs them all. So we fix our eyes not on what is seen, but on what is unseen, since what is seen is temporary, but what is unseen is eternal.

Even if our circumstances don't change, God can still change our hearts. Going through trials in faith allows Christlike virtues to become part of our everyday experience. The Scripture tells us that we must stay in God's process to see growth: "No discipline seems pleasant at the time, but painful. Later, however, it produces a harvest of righteousness and peace for those who have been trained by it" (Heb 12:11).

God Knows What to Do Next

We determine the type of relationship we have with God. In fact, he tries to have a closer relationship with us, but our reluctance to trust and obey hinders our nearness to him. When we go through trials, we sometimes think God doesn't value our relationship. And because we are experiencing strain it leads us to assume we have somehow fallen out of his favor. But experiencing trials doesn't mean God loves us any less. It simply means that our trials are opportunities for God to uphold us in his strength.

Knowing we are blameless in Christ gives us assurance that we have not fallen out of God's favor. Now, if it's true that we have God's approval, what does it mean when we suffer hardships? It means God will be with us in the trial. And that the Comforter will walk along side of us. It's encouraging to know that God wants to help in our time of need and make sure we receive strength for the journey.

Circumstances don't have to improve when God is by our side. And when he is by our side, his favor remains upon us. Knowing this gives us confidence that he is not trying to punish us with difficulties. God wants us to know that we have immeasurable worth, and he does not take pleasure in our misery. Instead, he desires that we grow from our challenges.

Our faith is weakened when we think God doesn't care about our struggles. That he sits high in the heavens, isolated and detached from what concerns us. But this is not the case. When Jesus was on earth, he showed how highly God valued our lives (Matt 10:29–31).

Yes, God cares about our troubles. It's just that he knows what's best for us. And even though it may not make sense now, we must step out in faith and trust that God knows what he's doing.

Many times, we try to remove discomfort from our lives. However, we must allow God's comfort to bring us the peace we need. This means we must wait for him. The reason we wait is for our good, not because God needs time to think about what to do next. For he's never confused.

God's plan is not restricted by our limitations either. Just knowing that his power and wisdom reach beyond our circumstances gives us confidence. Surely, we can trust him because he alone reveals a successful path through our trials. And it's this path that leads to peace and happiness.

In Step with God

The journeys that each of us take ultimately lead to a day when we can fully reflect Christ's likeness. Not only will we be like Christ but we will also be able to worship God in his glory. This alone brings joy and happiness. However, these promises won't be completed until we are joined with God in heaven. But we have joy today knowing God is developing Christlike virtues in our lives every day.

When we don't reflect Christ perfectly, we can become discouraged. But God sees our heart and will help us get to our destiny. Sometimes, we can feel like we're not growing and become dissatisfied. Certainly, our growth can become stunted for many reasons. Mostly, it's because we haven't walked the path of trust and obedience that was revealed in our trials. And it's this path that must be traveled. Certainly, there's no other way to grow except by trusting God and obeying his will.

Growth slows when we aren't in step with God. That's not to say we don't love him. It simply means we are still in the refining process and there are areas that require attention. While in the refining process, we must remain on God's path. But his path is often revealed one step at a time. And when he's silent, we must wait in faith.

Having the Right Perspective

The refining process is perfect for turning our weaknesses into assets. Truly, the way we view our challenges needs to shift. To help us, God has provided everything we need to have a healthy perspective. A healthy perspective means we trust God and live by faith. But escaping trials is not the same as living in faith. Instead of trying to escape, we are to ask ourselves, "What does God want to show me by going through this?" Then we embrace the adversity trusting that God will make a way for us to endure.

In moments when we feel like we can't take another step, God's path will lead to restoration. And even though our circumstances may not change, God will make a way. He will meet us in our trials to bring refreshing, life, and peace.

As we surrender and seek God, we will find him drawing close to us. No longer will we look for temporary solutions to our problems. But will look for change that makes an eternal difference. We will also learn to surrender without holding anything back and no longer fear that God will put us in situations that require us to trust him.

Instead, we ask him to search our hearts and show us the doubt, distrust, and fear that need to be removed (Ps 139:23–24). Of course, we are not asking to go through more trials, but we take joy knowing every experience helps us grow and brings us closer to him.

Fulfillment in Christ

There are good reasons we should center our lives on Christ. For it's not possible to experience fulfillment apart from him. Despite what we might think, kindness and morality alone do not secure happiness. Sure, these things may contribute to our overall well-being, but they do not ensure there is a connection with God. Only Jesus provides that connection and gives life through the Spirit. And without Jesus and the life that comes through him, a relationship with God would not be possible and neither would true joy.

Our Christian experience can be one of peace, love, and hope. Certainly, life doesn't always have to be bitter and sorrowful. As we continue to seek Jesus, he will provide what we need to have a satisfying life. But this means we must learn to be content with God's provision.

If Jesus is the source of our happiness, our fulfillment will never fade. And when we remain dependent on Christ, our joy will last forever. Jesus said in John 6:35, "I am the bread of life. Whoever comes to me will never go hungry, and whoever believes in me will never be thirsty."

Contentment stems from our trust in God. We trust him because we know he will provide for our needs. And that gives us peace. Even when he doesn't seem to respond, we wait with hope knowing God himself will be enough.

God is in our now moments. He wants to draw us near and help us understand his love. Sometimes, we forget that God's promises are for us right now. Sure, we'll be close to God once we get to heaven, but we can be close with him today, even in ordinary circumstances. Although God's kingdom has not yet arrived on earth, it can rule in our hearts. This means God desires to have a personal relationship with his people. He wants to know us, and we are to know him.

Recognize Where We Are

We often have our own ideas about how trials should end, or how challenges should be resolved. However, God is not like us; his ways are above our own. And sometimes, it doesn't make sense why God leads us down certain paths. But even if it doesn't make sense, we can trust that our circumstances will eventually work out for our good.

If adversity is part of God's plan, then we are to take joy knowing that we will have his help. Admittedly, some troubles are more difficult to endure than others. But regardless of the struggle, our focus is to be on fulfilling God's will for our life (John 21:22).

We don't give an accurate representation of the kingdom when we're unhappy with life. Romans 14:17 says, "For the kingdom of God is not a matter of eating and drinking, but of righteousness, peace and joy in the Holy Spirit." As believers, we don't just experience this peace and joy when circumstances are in our favor. For we can have happiness and contentment every day, no matter what situation we face.

Sometimes, we don't recognize the extent of our peace and joy until we encounter difficulties. Not only do we find that we run short of these virtues, but we learn to recognize God's endless supply. This is how adversity points us toward the source of true happiness. It also teaches us that contentment comes from embracing God's faithfulness. And this causes our life to be filled with peace and joy.

God doesn't want us facing problems by ourselves. Truly, we are never alone even if it feels like our troubles have overtaken us. Our problems may seem overwhelming, but God said he would provide a way for us to withstand the pressure. When our strength is gone, God wants us to know that he's with us. And he is enough!

Scriptures

chapter 1: Experiencing Joy Every Day
Exodus 20:11
1 Chronicles 16:34
Psalm 86:5
Proverbs 10:22
Isaiah 55:8
Mark 7:21
Romans 8:10–11
Hebrews 4:10

chapter 2: God's Process to Help Us
Romans 8:11
2 Corinthians 5:17
Galatians 3:14
Ephesians 1:3
Colossians 3:1

chapter 3: Acknowledging God's Goodwill
Deuteronomy 31:6
Isaiah 26:3
Matthew 5:6, 17:20
John 15:5
Galatians 5:22–23
Colossians 1:9–10
1 Timothy 6:6

2 Timothy 1:7, 3:16–17
James 1:2–4
1 Peter 5:7

chapter 4: Happiness in God's Presence

Exodus 40:34–35
2 Chronicles 7:1–3
Psalm 1:1–3, 34:18
Matthew 7:1, 13:45–46
Mark 10:24–25
Luke 6:45, 7:40–47, 10:30–37
John 4:19, 6:44
2 Corinthians 6:16
Hebrews 8:10
Revelation 1:17

chapter 5: Trials Are Part of God's Plan

Psalm 71:5
Matthew 4:1, 17:7, 19:26, 26:42
2 Corinthians 12:9
Ephesians 4:24
Philippians 4:13
Hebrews 11:6
Revelation 21:3

chapter 6: Do We Trust God?

Numbers 14:6–9
Proverbs 17:3
Matthew 6:34
Acts 16:25
Romans 8:28
1 John 4:9–10

chapter 7: Strengthened to Endure Challenges

Exodus 34:14
Proverbs 25:4
Mark 4:38, 14:1

Luke 10:30–37
John 11:1–44

chapter 8: God's Faithfulness Revealed
Job 25–26
Matthew 5:8, 44
Romans 8:35–39
Philippians 3:14
Hebrews 4:1–11
1 John 3:2
Jude 1:21
Revelation 21:4

chapter 9: God's Promises Are True
Matthew 9:19–22, 10:39, 15:13
John 3:16
Romans 8:11

chapter 10: Jesus Shows Us How to Follow God's Will
Exodus 14:16
Jeremiah 29:13
Matthew 19:16–26
Mark 2:17, 6:52, 15:34
John 4:34
1 Thessalonians 4:3
Hebrews 11:1–3

chapter 11: Fulfillment When Completely Surrendered
1 Samuel 16:7
Job 3, 13:15
Proverbs 9:10
Isaiah 29:13
Mark 8:33, 12:44
Luke 1:49, 74, 4:18–19
John 17:21–23
1 Corinthians 15:22

Ephesians 2:10
Philippians 3:9
Colossians 1:28
James 1:5
1 Peter 1:6–7

chapter 12: Pursuing God in Faith

Matthew 4:4, 5:16
Luke 11:33, 14:26–33
John 1:18, 3:21, 4:14
Hebrews 4:15, 9:14

chapter 13: No Longer Looking for an Escape

Job 13:20–21
John 1:1–18
1 Thessalonians 5:19
2 Thessalonians 2:16–17
2 Timothy 2:21
1 Peter 1:5, 3:12

chapter 14: Having Confidence in God

Psalm 55:22, 139:23–24
Matthew 10:29–31
John 5:8, 6:35, 21:22
Romans 5:3–5, 8:24, 14:17
2 Corinthians 4:7–10, 16–18
Philippians 4:7
Hebrews 12:11
1 Peter 1:8